TAKE BACK THE TRAY

TAKE BACK THE TRAY

Revolutionizing Food in Hospitals,
Schools, and Other Institutions

JOSHNA MAHARAJ

Published by ECW Press
665 Gerrard Street East
Toronto, Ontario, Canada M4M 1Y2
416-694-3348 / info@ecwpress.com

Editor for the Press: Jennifer Knoch
Cover design: Jessica Albert
Cover images: Photographs by Angus Fergusson, food styling by Haley Polinsky
Author photo: Melissa Yu Vanti

LIBRARY AND ARCHIVES CANADA CATALOGUING IN PUBLICATION

Title: Take back the tray : revolutionizing food in hospitals, schools, and other institutions / Joshna Maharaj.

Names: Maharaj, Joshna, author.

Description: Includes bibliographical references.

Identifiers: Canadiana (print) 20200153064
Canadiana (ebook) 20200153072

ISBN 978-1-77041-491-4 (softcover)
ISBN 978-1-77305-486-5 (PDF)
ISBN 978-1-77305-485-8 (ePUB)

Subjects: LCSH: Food service. | LCSH: Hospitals — Food service. | LCSH: Universities and colleges — Food service. | LCSH: Maharaj, Joshna — Anecdotes. | LCSH: Food service employees — Anecdotes.

Classification: LCC TX943 .M34 2020
DDC 642/.5—dc23

The publication of *Take Back the Tray* has been funded in part by the Government of Canada. *Ce livre est financé en partie par le gouvernement du Canada.* We acknowledge the contribution of the Government of Ontario through the Ontario Book Publishing Tax Credit, and through Ontario Creates for the marketing of this book.

PRINTED AND BOUND IN CANADA   PRINTING: FRIESENS 5 4 3 2

MIX
Paper from
responsible sources
FSC
www.fsc.org   FSC® C016245

For Gurudev, who saw it all and told a teenaged me that I would learn to be a very good cook . . . long before I ever had the idea myself.

CONTENTS

INTRODUCTION

"Food is the single strongest lever to optimize human health and environmental sustainability on Earth."
— EAT-LANCET COMMISSION ON HEALTHY DIETS
FROM SUSTAINABLE FOOD SYSTEMS

In the winter of 2019, I had a minor surgery on my sinuses. When I woke from the anaesthetic, my nose and my throat were burning with pain from the removed breathing tube, and I asked for ice chips to hold at the back of my throat for some relief. A short while later, I felt much more awake and was sitting upright when a nurse asked me what I wanted to eat: a ham and cheese or egg salad sandwich? After having fasted all morning for the surgery, I was starving and settled on an egg salad sandwich and a cold ginger ale over ice. What I really wanted was something that was cool and easy to swallow — some sorbet or even just some cold applesauce.

I had a pretty good idea of what to expect from that egg salad — it's one of the greatest hits of institutional food service after all — but this was the worst one yet: hard-cooked eggs, chopped and combined with some low-calorie whipped salad dressing (never mayonnaise), and a whisper of salt and pepper smooshed between two slices of perpetually soft and brilliantly white industrial sandwich bread that stuck to the roof of my mouth. The bread wasn't stale, because it was never really fresh. That stodgy bread is hard to swallow on a good day, and for my dry, raw, post-surgery throat, it was even more difficult. The eggs boasted the listless, pale yellow yolks of factory farmed eggs, which come from hens living in a confined, caged space, often nestled in their own waste and given antibiotics prophylactically. The shells of these eggs are very thin and break quite easily, because factory farmed birds don't live a full, active, healthy enough life to produce eggs with orange yolks and thick shells. The egg salad I make has scallions, parsley, and lemon juice in it for colour, crunch, and great flavour — all of which were nowhere to be found in this sandwich.

I'm pretty outspoken about my dislike for dry corners on a sandwich (I'll fire people for not spreading sandwich filling to the furthest edges of the crust), but this sandwich took dry corners to a whole new level. There was a one-inch dry barrier around the scant couple of tablespoons of egg salad that actually made it into the sandwich. It was served cold from the fridge, still wrapped in plastic marked with a Monday sticker (it was a Tuesday), which promised reasonable "freshness." But the honest truth is that there was hardly anything perishable in that egg salad sandwich, and it would have lasted much longer than the allotted three days. Nothing perishable ultimately means little to no real nutrition, just empty, unsatisfying calories. After I forced back my first bite, chasing it with cold, syrupy ginger ale from a Styrofoam cup, I looked at the other folks around me, having much the same experience. We were dopey, we were sore, and we were hungry. That sandwich did not say, "Get well soon!" That sandwich said, "Sorry, sucker, this is all they'll pay for."

I am a firm believer that any plate of food, served anywhere, is a reflection of the attitude and values that produced that plate. When you're in an award-winning, fine-dining restaurant, you can safely expect to be served food that is prepared with expert skill. When you've just returned home from work and someone has already started cooking dinner, you know that you're getting a meal that comes with some care and affection. The dismal tray of reheated food that is placed in front of hospital patients three times a day tells them that they are not worth any more effort. We know you're sick, we know you need to heal, but this is as far as we're going to go to nourish your body back to health.

It's no big revelation to say that institutional food is not good. Hospital food is famously ridiculed, chronic student hunger is deemed a rite of passage, and prison meals are considered part of the punishment. And while there are countless well-intentioned folks working in institutions everywhere, doing the very best they can with what they've got, the meals generally remain quite tasteless and are made with the most highly processed ingredients available for the lowest possible price. The majority of kitchens in institutions have become dusty storage areas, with most food housed in massive freezers and prepared using reheating units. It wasn't always this way. At The Scarborough Hospital in Toronto, there is a wood-panelled fridge with sharp hooks that used to hang sides of beef for butchering on-site. In 2011, that fridge was used exclusively to chill and set Jell-O.

But we can do better. I know this because I've spent the last 14 years as a chef and activist on the front lines trying to rebuild institutional food systems. I've led projects in three types of public institutions: community food centres, hospitals, and universities. Other institutions are part of this conversation too. Institutional feeding happens in elementary and secondary schools, long-term care facilities, and prisons. Prisons are the only institutions that are seen as places for punishment, but if rehabilitation is the goal, food that restores health and dignity is essential.

From all of the work I've done, conversations I've had, and stories I've heard, it always seems to come down to the same thing: nobody with any real power cares enough about food to do anything differently. There is a lack of collective understanding about the role that good food plays in supporting health and well-being, education, and rehabilitation. If we truly understood how vital it is to invest in our food systems and, ultimately, ourselves, we wouldn't make it such a low priority. This is a story about the deep disconnection between people and their food.

What I'm trying to do with my work is lift both our food budgets and priorities out of the gutter. I'm trying to rework the ill-informed, dismissive attitude that allowed, and even encouraged, the chopping of those budgets in the first place. The most important consideration for institutional food should *not* be how much it costs; prioritizing low spending over proper feeding is precisely what has gotten us into this mess. Food has the ability to improve our health and wellness, but these cheap, lifeless, industrial menus are not nourishing anyone — and they're contributing to the climate crisis. Access to good, nutritious food is a basic human right, not a luxury.

Now, it's important to note that my purpose here is not to point fingers or blame individual hospitals, schools, or long-term care facilities. The responsibility for these problems lies with an institutional culture that holds food at a very low priority. This culture is partly the result of a slow death by a thousand budget cuts over the last couple of decades and of the tone set by government. At some point in our history, we decided that it was simply too expensive to pay a real human being to stand at a kitchen counter and prepare fresh meals on-site from scratch every day. And now, make no mistake, friends, we have gotten what we've paid for.

The obvious villain in all this is industrial food, which has only been around since just after the Second World War, when a number of factors came together, like a Betty Crocker cake from a box. Military innovations in packaged, non-perishable food were shared with commercial producers, which made them widely available and affordable — you can thank Uncle Sam for microwaves, boxed mac and cheese, instant coffee, and so much more. Women joined the workforce in larger numbers, meaning less time for scratch cooking. Innovation in pesticides and herbicides supported monoculture farming and an expansion of commodity crops that were the building blocks of convenience foods. In a booming post-war economy, food became a status symbol: like a dress or a table, an imported, store-bought thing was more glamorous than homemade. And let's not forget the explosion of advertising, which promised women liberation from the kitchen via TV dinners, cold cereals, and canned soup.

The real potential of industrial food was realized in public institutions, for which this affordable packaged food seemed like a dream come true: a whole catalogue of frozen prepared foods that could be resurrected with minimal labour and resources. As the bottom line became the highest priority, budgets got tighter.

But it is critical to recognize that the highly processed industrial food we're buying and serving is artificially cheap, and that the planet, taxpayers, and people of the developing world are picking up the tab. Raj Patel, a renowned academic, journalist, and good food activist, addresses this issue head-on in his book *The Value of Nothing*. Patel argues that our narrow focus on price (for things like consumer goods) prevents us from acknowledging the hidden costs of production. While the average cost of a Big Mac is about $4, he cites a report by the Centre for Science and the Environment in India, which speculates that the price tag for a Big Mac, with beef raised in clear-cut forests, is closer to $200. These costs, or externalities, are massive and largely unarticulated, so let's spend a bit of time on them.

First, there's the impact on our physical environment: the waterways contaminated by fertilizer run-off or the industrial sludge of feedlot waste, the land degraded by persistent monocropping, the oil turned into packaging that piles up in landfills and the bellies of sea creatures, and the carbon heating of the atmosphere resulting from shipping food all over the planet. Second, there are the costs of food subsidies. In many parts of the Western world, certain agricultural cash crops, such as corn, soy, and wheat, are subsidized by governments and thus inexpensive for industry to feed to animals in feedlots or to turn into refined carbs, high-fructose corn syrup, and other industrial food staples. The food isn't cheaper — it's partially prepaid, and we, the consumer, aren't paying the full cost. Third, there are social subsidies. Consider the underpaid and often-exploited migrant labourers required to work long, gruelling days in feedlots, slaughterhouses, and farmer's fields. And what about those in the service industry dishing up these chemical confections? Those low menu prices do not pay a living wage; in fact, a 2019 report on worker-pay disparity in the fast food industry revealed that a CEO makes 1,000 times what an average full-time worker makes. This leaves working people in the frustrating position of still requiring some form of social assistance to get through the month.

And, finally, there are public health costs connected to highly processed foods, which do not contain adequate amounts of nutrition. Consider the powdered "beef" broth that is a staple in institutional kitchens: 14 ingredients, none of which, curiously, are beef — yes, most commercial powdered beef broth is technically vegetarian. The texture of this broth is thin, lacking the rich gelatinousness of real broth made from beef bones. The flavour is weak: miscellaneous "seasoning" with a hint of beefiness. And while it has been common knowledge for many generations around the world that broth is restorative, and the right thing to serve to sick people, there is nothing in this particular broth that will make anyone feel good. A cup of hot water would do a better job.

A recent study from the University of Montreal links chronic disease to highly processed foods, which are high in calories, sugars, sodium, and saturated fats. "Not only do ultra-processed foods not contribute to a healthy diet, but they displace other healthier foods that do," said report author Jean-Claude Moubarac, an assistant professor of nutrition at the University of Montreal. This is a really important bit to remember. The highly processed industrial food on our institutional menus, particularly in hospitals, is not only unappetizing, low-nutrition, and laden with a constellation of external costs, but it comes at the expense of the good, wholesome foods that our bodies actually need. In fact, Statistics Canada reported in 2017 that only 30 percent of Canadian adults consume the recommended five or more servings of fruits and vegetables each day. As Dr. Edward Xie wrote in the *National Observer*, "No pills or surgery will fix a poor diet."

Tyler Norris, a vice president at American non-profit health care company Kaiser Permanente, put it succinctly at a conference hosted by the Sustainable Food Trust: "If you are in the food sector, you are also in the health sector." He further warned that "the multiple externalities of cheap empty calories, and the food system that delivers them, are reflected in declining population health status and, in turn, in higher health care costs. Cheap calories are not so cheap in the long run."

Since these calories are both the most affordable and the most commonly provided at food banks, the health burden of industrial food falls disproportionately on low-income families, who are also disproportionately people of colour. According to Canada Without Poverty, one in five racialized families live in poverty, as opposed to one in 20 white families. "Controlling food is a means of controlling power," said Sean Sherman, an Oglala Lakota chef in the U.S. who is using food to further decolonization and education. He reminds us of the rapidly shrinking access to wholesome, culturally appropriate foods for Indigenous people, at the hands of colonizing settlers. Denying people access to the food they need not just to survive but to thrive limits their potential and contributes to oppressive systems remaining unchallenged. For many people, a hospital stay is an unwelcome detour into industrial eating, but for others it is a daily reality.

I remember standing in the atrium of one of Toronto's hospitals and looking through the pamphlets with impressive glossy, full-colour photos and lots of talk about the "boundless vistas of innovation and excellence" that were being explored by their medical care. They also boasted about the world-class calibre of doctors, surgeons, nurses, and other medical professionals who worked in the hospital. These folks were bright, focused, and committed to outstanding patient care. The pamphlet made it clear: the hospital was shooting for greatness. Why, then, were they *choosing* not to apply that same attitude towards food service? Consider the money allocated for food ingredients in hospitals: currently in Canada, we spend between $8 and $15 per patient per day for three meals and a snack. In Ontario, the use of a hospital bed for one night is about $842. These two numbers alone show a huge disparity between what we spend to house and treat a patient and what we spend to feed a patient. It's safe to say that the current model is really the bare minimum required to put meals on trays. The proof, you might say, is in the pudding cup.

The truth is the issue with institutional food is not actually the food. Rather, the real problem is that the wrong attitudes and values are currently guiding institutional food service. As it stands, the main values being served by institutional food are fiscal responsibility, profit generation, and contract compliance. What I'm looking for is a major culture change. I want institutions to bring health, humanity, and hospitality back to food while also building sustainability, supporting the local economy, and reinvigorating the work of frontline staff. This isn't about finding a new supplier and some fresh recipes; this is about new habits and an attitude shift. There are no quick fixes that last, and we are not going to shop our way out of this one.

Now, it's important to say that if you are looking for a plan that lowers costs for institutional food service, you will not find that here. Although I've found ways to provide good food frugally, the idea that real, wholesome food should cost less than the current "edible, food-like substances," as writer Michael Pollan calls them, is ridiculous. A return to sustainably sourced, scratch-made food only seems to be expensive because we have dramatically reduced what we're willing to invest in food. In most cases, food service budgets are just a fraction of their former selves. The good news is there are huge holistic benefits, including economic ones, to these changes — we just need to expand our focus beyond the bottom line.

Most of this book is about all the exciting things that are possible when we aim higher. So, let's lay out some new guiding values. I believe food in public institutions should be:

- Wholesome, affordable, and delicious
- Deeply nourishing, with seasonal menus

- Made from scratch, on-site every day
- Made with thought and care by a skilled worker with a good, secure job
- Made with organic ingredients that are locally produced
- Reflective of the cultural diversity of the community
- Accessible for people with dietary restrictions, be they cultural, medical, or personal
- Purchased via a network that is transparent, fair, and just
- A vitally necessary part of the high standard of care and service offered in the institution

The values that guide the meals should be the same ones that guide the rest of the organization. We need to put those principles back into the meals we serve in hospitals, schools, and prisons. Taking the time to choose and articulate what matters is as important for a public institution as it is for an individual or a household. You can't assert your values if you don't first know what they are. And right now, in public institutions, food is not a priority, it's an irritating necessity.

Change in institutions is anything but easy. They're built to do one thing, one way. And if you want to change one element of the way an institution functions, you have to be ready to change a number of other things about the operating processes to actually make it work. It's like pulling a thread or knocking down a line of dominoes. If patients were being well fed by accountant-driven budgets and if students were well nourished on campuses, I wouldn't be calling for significant changes to the system. But that is not the case, and the very real truth is that the current system is simply not working: we're not meeting the needs of the people we're supposed to be taking care of and we're wasting both food and money under the guise of efficiency. We can do so much better.

This is a revolution that needs us all: policy makers, administrators, teachers, health care providers, activists, chefs, and anyone who has felt the sting of institutional food, either first-hand or via someone they love. It's for patients, residents, students, prisoners, and their communities. This book is for people who care about food and who care about where our society is headed. Because can't we tell the most about a society from how it cares for its vulnerable?

This isn't just my work, it's personal, and it should be personal for you too. While my hospital stay was limited to that one day, I have visited people in the hospital with food in hand many times. I remember when my family spent the better part of a week in the ICU, scared and worrying about a beloved aunt whose health had taken a sudden turn for the worse. It was awful enough that we all had to face the fact that the end of her life was coming much sooner than anybody had thought, and the dry, expensive sandwiches available at the on-site café did little to nourish or soothe anyone. I've discovered that worry really rattles around uncomfortably with hunger, and the only thing worse than worrying about the health of someone you love is doing so on an empty stomach. So, I'd arrive every day with fresh food that actually fed our bodies and gave everyone a small but much-needed boost.

After my first hospital project, my dad had a pacemaker installed. After he woke up from the anaesthetic, they brought him a dinner tray, and my dad lifted that dome to reveal a slapped-together square of lasagne with a limp green salad. He looked at me, then put the dome back down and lifted it again, and I could see in his eyes that he was really hoping there would be something different, and more appetizing, under there the second time around. He looked down at that food, then up at me and asked, "So, you haven't gotten around to this place yet, huh?" I get photos sent to me all the time, from my people and from strangers, of the terrible meals in a hospital or the sad, half-hearted food that their kids are being served in their residence cafeterias. Something that I hadn't thought about was the experience of my fellow chefs who have been in the hospital themselves, or with a loved one. One chef told me about the frustrating pain of his grandmother's last days. She fed her whole family for a lifetime and inspired him to become a cook, and the last meals of her life were dismal hospital trays.

And while I haven't had any experience working in a prison, an inmate's partner emailed me about the meal service there. The menus were actually quite similar to what we see in hospitals and schools. The real difference was in the way the food was served: this inmate reported that what was on the menu and what actually showed up on the plates was rarely the same thing, and any time a question was asked about this, they were told to shut up and eat what they were given or eat nothing. And it gets worse: according to non-profit news organization the Marshall Project, some prisoners are fed only twice a day and often left hungry. In one Arizona prison, the average price per meal per inmate was a mere $0.56. And, according to a study from the Centers for Disease Control and Prevention, lax food safety also makes a prisoner six times more likely to be hit with foodborne illness. While I don't suppose that this is much of a surprise, I stand by my conviction: no institution should condone a style of food service that humiliates and dehumanizes a person.

This book is not a definitive guide to rebuilding institutional food. I haven't figured it all out by any stretch of the imagination. Instead, this book identifies what's not working and offers some tools, experience, and inspiration to chart a new way forward. I am convinced that a better life is on the other side of this . . . for *all* of us. With a sustained commitment from all levels of society — from federal leadership right down to the person dealing with a kitchen's waste — real change is very possible. I have ventured into the belly of the beast a few times now, and even though I haven't figured it all out, I have pieced together some of it, and this is what I'm sharing with you. I am confident we can do a better job of feeding people in hospitals, schools, and prisons, and I know there is a way to use food to make actual change in our institutions and in our world. The revolution starts in the kitchen, friends, and I'm delighted to tell you that it tastes delicious.

CHAPTER 1

GOOD FOOD VALUES

"People will forget what you said, forget what you did,
but people will never forget how you made them feel."
— MAYA ANGELOU, POET

Before we get into specific case studies from my time on the ground, I want to first unpack two core principles that guide my work as a chef: hospitality and sustainability.

Hospitality is generally defined as the relationship between host and guest. It's a warm welcome and an offering of nourishment and comfort. There is hospitality in thoughtful, attentive service and a well-set table. For people working in the food and restaurant industry, hospitality is a guiding priority, though I feel it's often not fully understood. Ultimately, hospitality is about humanity: it's a relationship between the person serving the food and the person receiving; it's anticipating needs and offering kindness, usually in the form of a good meal. Hospitality lets food service workers be caregivers and thus sets the stage for others to feel cared for. Farm-fresh food cooked from scratch with care and attention requires a lot of human effort to pull off, and through my work in public institutions over the years, I have realized that hospitality, or this human connection, has been deemed too expensive and ultimately unnecessary by people looking to trim budgets. The storms of budget cuts that have rained down on institutions over the last couple of decades have washed hospitality into the gutter and, with it, the fundamental idea that you, as a person, matter.

New York restauranteur Danny Meyer talks about hospitality as a conversation, where hosts anticipate the needs of their guests in the interest of offering a meaningful, restorative experience. He believes that our first experience of hospitality is at birth, when we receive the "first four gifts of life: eye contact, a smile, a hug, and some food." What I really love about this idea is that it positions hospitality as one of the most simple, basic elements of life. It's connection, kindness, affection, and nourishment. Hospitality is not about a beautiful dining room or the most exquisitely prepared food. In fact, one of my most vivid memories of great hospitality was a lunch I ate under a tree, sitting cross-legged on a burlap runner on the grass and using my hands to eat a simple preparation of lentils, rice, and vegetables off a stainless steel plate. We receive hospitality from the earth and from each other, but hospitality does not happen automatically. You have to choose to offer it; you have to decide that it is important enough to invest in.

Very often, we talk about the importance of good service in the context of restaurants, and in many cases we even tip for it, but the truth is solely focusing on the service leaves you with only half the story and a missed opportunity. In his book *Setting the Table*, Danny Meyer explains, "Service is the technical delivery of a product. Hospitality is how the delivery of that product makes its recipient feel. Service is a monologue — we decide how we want to do things and set our own standards for service. Hospitality, on the other hand, is a dialogue. To be on a guest's side requires listening to that person with every sense, and following up with a thoughtful, gracious, appropriate response. It takes both great service and great hospitality to rise to the top." I can attest to the fact that this man is walking his talk. Every time I'm in New York, I feel compelled to try the newest, hottest thing, hunting for flavour and style ideas . . . and without fail, I find myself with a reservation at Gramercy Tavern, one of Meyer's restaurants. Every subsequent visit after my first, I have been greeted with a "welcome back!" from the host staff at the door, and one year they even asked how I was enjoying the cookbook that I had purchased the previous summer. At the front of the dining room, there is a glorious table filled with the most enticing display of seasonal produce and foliage, and I am often just as excited about seeing that table as I am about eating! The food is consistently thoughtful and delicious, and the team does such an incredible job of making you feel so good, you can't help but go back. It's a great illustration of French food writer Jean Anthelme Brillat-Savarin's definition of hospitality: "To invite people to dine with us is to make ourselves responsible for their well-being for as long as they are under our roofs."

The slashing of budgets has largely meant the elimination of hospitality from institutional food service, and ultimately the elimination of human connection. That lacklustre tray of food and a campus food court full of global franchises tells patients and students that they are not worth any more effort than this, shitty meal after shitty meal. This is certainly not good service, and it dehumanizes and disappoints. But hospitality is not only pleasant, it inherently maintains dignity. Early in my career, I learned that if you treat each patron with the same level of welcome and generosity, you do not have to do any extra work to maintain the self-worth of your guests. This is why it makes so much sense to me that chefs with a solid foundation of hospitality should be the ones to move into institutional spaces to rebuild food service.

The second principle, sustainability, is more complex. The term itself has been overused, but in the context of food, sustainability is primarily concerned with our relationship with our physical environment. It's about how we work the land to produce food, how we move food from field to kitchen to table, how we handle waste, and how we manage the resources to make this all happen. A sustainable approach to food and cooking deeply respects the land and its resources, ensuring that there will be enough for all, forever.

Curiously, most sustainability initiatives within institutions, in my experience, are focused on waste management and on resource, energy, and chemical use. It is quite possible that things have changed since I was on the ground in an institution, but at the time, the connection between food services and sustainability was not obvious. The truth is there are many points of intersection here. First is the way we source food: how it is grown and where it comes from. Second is the physical maintenance of the kitchen: managing waste, how we use water, how much disposable material we use, and, of course, emptying that grease trap. Third is how we serve meals to guests: are the disposables we use biodegradable? How do we use energy in the dining room? Who does the laundry? And finally, there's the admin. This is stuff like our cost-to-income ratio, our expenses, and our connections to other kitchens and the community beyond the walls of our space. This constellation of elements all contribute to making an operation viable, but I think we need to explicitly include them in our understanding of sustainability. Can we continue to do things this way perpetually into the future? Sustainability is about encouraging staff to minimize waste, respect food ingredients and resources, and search for ways to make systems more efficient, less wasteful, and more connected.

When planning a menu, one of my first considerations is the ingredients. The idea of eating locally has been around for as long as we've been eating, but the word "locavore" didn't appear in print until 2005. Since then, the concept of eating locally has found international support, gaining prominence and momentum in the last 10 to 15 years, especially as dealing with the climate crisis becomes more urgent. For me, local food is food that is grown within a day's drive of where you live. The produce has ripened on the vine, in the sunshine, and is at its nutritional and flavour peak when it is harvested for market. But beyond flavour and nutrition, eating locally is about supporting different financial networks. Buying food that is grown where you live dramatically closes the gap between producer and consumer, while also making financial investments in local agriculture. A 2015 report by the Greenbelt Foundation revealed Ontario currently imports $20 billion worth of food each year, and 50 percent of that imported food could be produced in Ontario. Prioritizing agriculture and local production could result in an additional $10 billion in income for our province's food sector. My friends at the Greenbelt tell me that for every dollar spent initially in the farm sector, a total of $2.24 circulates throughout the economy.

But even with all of these compelling factors, the most important thing about local food is that it substantially reduces the amount of fossil fuels burned in moving it to its end point. Here's the model for imported food: produce is picked while still unripe and packed into cardboard cases on a truck; it's then moved to another part of the world by truck, ship, or plane, with the hope that it ripens en route. In the U.S., the average food item travels an astonishing 1,640 kilometres from factory or farm to store, or 6,760 kilometres when we take into account its entire supply chain (for example, transporting food to feed animals). This international shipping spree allows us to have menus that look the same all year, with bananas for our morning smoothies and a Caesar salad any time we want it. Food is treated like a commodity, a consumer good that can be manipulated to serve our needs. Imported food is reliably underripe and low in flavour. The fruit especially is always quite sour, and to be honest, I can't blame it.

Shipping food globally is just one way our food system relies on so many practices that don't factor into a sustainable future: there's also single use paper and plastic; raising meat in feedlot farms; growing thousands of hectares of one crop; overusing fertilizers, pesticides, and herbicides; and consuming a staggering amount of bottled water. Our desire to eat whatever we want, whenever we want, for the lowest possible price is fuelling the ravenous monster that is the climate crisis, and we need to change our behaviour before it's too late.

The writing is on the wall, friends. The August 2019 report from the Intergovernmental Panel on Climate Change (IPCC) notes that 21 to 37 percent of man-made greenhouse gas emissions come from the global food system. We also waste more than a quarter of the food we produce, which not only is a tragic waste considering the over 800 million people who are hungry each year but also contributes to 10 percent of anthropogenic greenhouse gas emissions. In fact, global research organization

Project Drawdown has identified preventing food waste as the third most effective climate intervention: something that could prevent 70.53 gigatons of CO_2 from entering the atmosphere by 2050. Let's not forget.that growing food also gets more difficult in a warming world: the IPCC report notes that "climate change exacerbates land degradation through increases in rainfall intensity, flooding, drought frequency and severity, heat stress, wind, sea-level rise, and wave action." To make matters worse, the food that we're growing is offering fewer nutrients. IPCC experiments suggest that wheat grown at higher CO_2 levels contains less protein, zinc, and iron, and a May 2019 study of 10 global food crops determined we've already seen a 1 percent decrease in caloric density thanks to climate change.

How food is grown is also a big consideration in ecological impact. Though we're getting more familiar with the term "organic," until now, as eaters, our thinking about organic food has been exclusively about us and what we want (or don't want) to put in our bodies. But the truth is there's much more to organic farming than this. According to the Rodale Institute, organic farming is done with "no synthetic pesticides and inputs, which disrupt soil life, and fossil-fuel dependent nitrogen fertilizer," and that's usually what comes to mind when we hear the term "organic." But there's another side to this that is about consciously nurturing the land and helping restore its natural systems and resilience. Many of our modern farming methods used in large-scale, chemical-intensive agriculture can actually degrade the soil up to 100 times faster than the soil can regenerate, which spells trouble for future food crops. Organic agriculture often includes regenerative agriculture practices like crop rotation, composting, residue mulching, no-till growing, and cover cropping, which restore nutrients to the soil so that it can continue to produce food indefinitely. Project Drawdown notes that 50 percent of the soil's carbon has been released into the atmosphere in previous centuries, but regenerative agriculture allows us to sequester that carbon and use it to grow food, what Drawdown calls "one of the greatest opportunities to address human and climate health, along with the financial well-being of farmers." And for bottom-line lovers, an investment of $57 billion in regenerative agriculture could mean a return of $1.9 trillion by 2050. With facts like these and the escalating climate crisis, it makes sense to me that an agricultural practice that reverses some of the impact should be a priority. Public institutions are in a perfect position to take leadership on supporting regenerative agriculture by investing their food dollars in farms and farmers who grow this way.

When asked whether local or organic is more important, I generally respond by saying that local trumps organic. I'd much rather people eat local, conventional food than imported organic food. My friends Brent Preston and Gillian Flies at The New Farm in Creemore, Ontario, would disagree, as they're firm believers that local and organic must go together and that conventional growing needs to be phased out as an option. And I completely agree with them. We *should* all be eating local, organic food grown on a small family farm. This is the food that I believe is a basic human right.

But in institutions, I'm making the case for a return to scratch cooking after years of cutting open packages of dried and frozen food, and I've been told by administrators that I would not be able to get agreement and action on scratch cooking, local eating, *and* organic sourcing in our first move. I think massive transitions require multiple points of entry depending on where people are at. My job as the leader is to assert the values and nurture action that will get everyone's feet pointed in the same direction as we move forward towards our scratch-made, local, organic future.

In all the projects I've undertaken, hospitality — how we treat each other — and sustainability — how we treat the land — have been the foundation. Scratch-made, culturally diverse menus; comfortable, inviting dining spaces; and cheerful, informative signage are all about offering great hospitality. Purchasing policies, cleaning schedules, inventory management, and staff training are all about building sustainability. I'd even say that any food initiative looking to create some social change must have hospitality and sustainability as guiding values. If you're not leading with hospitality and sustainability in your work, you're likely not making much real positive change.

CHAPTER 2

COMMUNITY FOOD CENTRES

Getting Started at The Stop

"Everybody gotta eat right, yo."
— COMMON, RAPPER, AUTHOR, AND ACTIVIST

On a late summer Saturday afternoon in 2008, the sun was high overhead, shining down on roughly 200 folks in a backyard garden in the west end of Toronto. People chatted around tables topped with bouquets of wildflowers, kids darted playfully through the crowd, and servers with trays of hors d'oeuvres and swirls of cocktail napkins offered guests delicious, seasonal mouthfuls that had been prepared by a chef with ingredients right from the garden. There was a smooth, tangy beet purée on a rice crisp with a topping of crunchy sprouts, and ribbons of grilled flank steak nestled into a roasted tomato salsa on top of a crostini. Sautéed mushrooms replaced the steak for a veg option, and mini chicken tostadas were garnished with a spicy, citrusy guacamole. A little while later, trays of spiced pear cake topped with a mascarpone cream appeared, and kids grinned over freshly baked cookies, full of seeds, whole grains, dried fruit, and chocolate chips. Guests sipped on infusions of herbs from the garden, and a folk band played, coaxing guests into dancing the afternoon away.

This might sound like any fancy, ticketed garden party, but the backyard garden was behind a community centre, the servers were volunteers, their trays were well-worn baking sheets, and the guests were all community members, many of whom were living with poverty, food insecurity, and a host of other vulnerabilities. This event, the Good Food for All Festival, was a celebration of a bountiful harvest and of another season of fun, engaging, and vital community programming at The Stop, a local community food centre.

"Community food centre" is a relatively new term that refers to a hub that provides its surrounding food-insecure community with increased access to good, wholesome, nutritious meals. You might not think of a grassroots community space as an institution, but I'll argue that this name fits quite nicely. Institutions can be a physical place like an office, restaurant, concert hall, or school, or an organization, such as the Red Cross or the Catholic Church. Institutions serve their communities, which often makes us think of government involvement, but The Stop is actually an organization that has stepped in to do something government can't or won't do — build community food security.

The Stop wasn't always a destination for glamorous garden parties. It started in the 1980s as a humble food bank operating out of a church basement. Since then, it has expanded its programming to include drop-in meals, a healthy food bank, perinatal programming, civic advocacy, accessibly priced fresh food markets, and community cooking and gardening programs. In 2018, they served 52,026 drop-in meals, had 1,551 visits to community kitchens, and grew over 2,000 pounds of fresh organic produce.

The job opening at The Stop was for a cook to make lunches twice a week and keep the kitchen running smoothly while simultaneously supporting organizational values around human rights, social justice, and sustainability. One of The Stop's foundational values is that access to good food is a basic human right. I was instantly drawn to the mission but worried that taking the job at The Stop might kill my culinary dreams, as there were no crisp white jackets down this road. But I was compelled enough by the opportunity, so I jumped in, reminding myself that though people don't pay for our meals, our kitchen should still operate at the same level as all other professional kitchens in the city.

There are a variety of reasons why people are food insecure, and most of them have to do with unequal and inequitable access to money and power. Whereas hunger is the physical and emotional sensation of needing to be fed, food security focuses on a person's or community's ability to feed that hunger. PROOF, a research team at the University of Toronto, reported in 2012 that one in eight Canadian households was food insecure. This amounted to 4 million people, including just over 1 million children. Numbers in the U.S. are similar, with one in eight Americans being food insecure in 2017, totalling 40 million people, including 12 million kids, according to non-profit Feeding America. These numbers are troubling enough, but there's something more important to recognize here and some assumptions to dissolve. Stereotypically, we think about food-insecure people as being homeless, unemployed, or both. But PROOF's 2012 report found that in Ontario, "over 60 percent of food-insecure households are relying on wages and salaries as their main source of income." It's not just that people are hungry, it's that working people cannot afford to feed themselves and their families properly, which is the signature of low-wage, precarious employment, in addition to poverty. In 2019, it is an absolute disgrace that hunger and food insecurity remain as prevalent as they do. It says a lot about our collective priorities that we all walk around with mini computers in our pockets, yet people still go to bed hungry.

What I love about The Stop is its deep understanding that when hunger hits, it has a domino effect on every other aspect of that person's life, and things fall quite rapidly. Effective community food security strategies need to be holistic and include emergency food programming, capacity building, and some type of a civic engagement or advocacy plan to allow vulnerable folks to advocate for themselves and each other. At The Stop, while people wait for a food bank hamper, they have the chance to speak to someone in a legal clinic about housing issues. After eating lunch at the drop-in, folks can join a community kitchen to build their cooking skills or head out to the garden to learn how to grow some of their own food.

Financial poverty is clearly the main problem, but a knowledge poverty also stands in the way of people accessing good food. It's one thing to not be able to afford proper nourishment, but it's a different thing to not know how to use raw ingredients to make something wholesome and delicious. Good cooking is about ingredients *and* skill, and we need to help people get both.

While I was in the food bank during my first couple weeks at The Stop, one of the community members told us that he lived in a rooming house and had only a microwave and a kettle to cook with. I searched the shelves and found a box of couscous and some other canned vegetables and wrote down a quick recipe for him. By the end of the day, I had had many conversations with people picking up hampers about the kinds of things they could cook with the food they were receiving. Rice, beans, carrots, and onions are cheap, but that doesn't mean anything if you don't know how to cook them. My years of running community kitchens and meal programs have taught me that unlocking cooking skills for people opens up opportunities for pleasure, nourishment, and self-reliance.

The kitchen at The Stop is a good size, with a big island in the centre; a large, powerful range; stainless steel counters with stacks of large pots, bowls, and hotel pans under-neath; and a commercial dishwasher. The bones of this kitchen are fantastic, and compared to most commercial kitchens, it's a luxurious amount of space. What was missing from this kitchen were systems and organization and a sense that someone was there to maintain the space in a way that could really support the programming. When I arrived, I started cleaning and organizing in the small pantry. I learned so much about how the kitchen was running by the state of affairs in the pantry. At that point in the organization's history, the food ingredients for programming almost exclusively came in via donations from a local food bank and a food rescue organization. Those organizations had large, centralized warehouses that received food from manufacturers, public donations, grocery stores, and other large corporations and delivered them to member agencies, like The Stop, a couple of times a week.

Cliff Gayer, the food bank coordinator would call me to join him outside when the truck arrived. We'd fill up carts with what was on offer that day, and I'd use this inventory to guide my menu creation for lunches for the rest of the week. It became very clear to me that this ecosystem was not one that supported very much scratch cooking. Off the truck, we got lots of bottled sauces and vinaigrettes, ready-made "salads" (usually carbs covered in mayo), tins of pasta sauce, lots of packaged snacks, and just-add-water packaged foods. One raw ingredient we did get was boxes of mixed frozen grocery store meats that were close to or just at their best-before date. There was never enough to actually cook a lunch with, so we'd keep pork, beef, and chicken bins in the freezer and collect these little bits until I had a large enough supply to cook with. On occasion, I would get lucky and there would be bags of rice, cans of whole tomatoes, blocks of cheese, and fresh or frozen vegetables. As the guys on the trucks got to know the kinds of things that I would take, they'd save special things for me because they knew that I was a chef and could use it. I'd get boxes of lovely mushrooms, good olive oil, and the occasional nice hunk of cheese to put towards a lunch or community kitchen session.

Despite these exceptions, I routinely found the ingredients I had to work with in direct conflict with my culinary philosophy: I feel that food should be scratch-made from good, whole ingredients. I wanted as much cultural diversity as possible and consistent accommodations for vegetarians. But most of all, I wanted our meals to be full of as much flavour and nutrition as I could pack in, as these lunches were often the only meals that our community members would eat in a day.

At this point, it's really important to note that drop-in centres and community kitchens are staffed almost exclusively by volunteers. In the non-profit world, resources are scarce, and staff need to be able to serve meals and snacks that can be prepared easily, with minimal time and equipment, often using whatever ingredients are available. Organizations generally don't have the space or labour to prepare scratch-made meals, so the pre-made, packaged stuff that comes off the donation trucks makes very light, doable work of getting meals out to community members. This said, we had a kitchen and a chef, and to me, that was a huge opportunity to do more than basic calorie delivery.

It is often said that beggars can't be choosers, and that hungry people should accept any food that is offered to them. I call bullshit. Hungry people still deserve to have their humanity and dignity preserved while accessing emergency food services. I was so grateful to have organizational values that supported this thinking. The Stop's mandate to serve food that is as wholesome and nutritious as possible allowed us to be choosy about what we took off the truck. It allowed us to say no to cases of pop, pudding that was supposed to taste like cotton candy, and other things with so little nutritional value that you'd need a chemistry degree to make them. As I've already mentioned, a diet of non-perishable food does not support real health and wellness. These foods are packed full of salt, sugar, and other preservatives that do little more than play tricks with your taste buds. The difference between the crispness of a fresh sautéed green bean and the soft, and often salty, defeated version that is locked in a can is night and day. I understand that sometimes that choice isn't available, and the can wins over hunger. Yet so many people continue to fill those donation bins in the grocery store, patting themselves on the back for being charitable and generous with the things they've pulled from the back of their cupboards and blown off the dust. The next time you are asked to contribute to a food drive, offer a cash donation to the organization so they can purchase good, perishable food to break the cycle of malnutrition that ensnares most food-insecure people.

Our work with vulnerable populations taught us without a doubt that malnutrition is a child of poverty: low-income folks often find themselves stuck consuming food that will more likely leave them diabetic than adequately nourished. Tom Boyce, chief of the University of California at San Francisco's Division of Developmental Medicine, confirms this link between income and hunger, saying, "Socioeconomic status is the most powerful predictor of disease, disorder, injury, and mortality we have." A global study by University of Washington's Institute of Health Metrics and Evaluation showed that poor diet is a factor in one in five deaths around the world, and that in 2016, 11 percent of the world's population was undernourished. Poverty is a slow death sentence, and consistent access to real, whole food is vital if we want to change outcomes for people living with poverty. At The Stop, our meals were an attempt to challenge the status quo because they were scratch-made with fresh ingredients. I wanted my kitchen, serving simple, wholesome food, to be a living example of how things could be done differently.

After the first year, I made the case for buying fresh salad greens, as they were items that never came in on the truck but very much needed to balance out our meals. I managed to get a small budget for lunch ingredients and this allowed me to make sure that there was a fresh salad on a quarter of each plate. I used the money to buy pre-washed salad greens, and we would use whatever vegetables we received from the truck and from our own organic garden during its growing season. Instead of taking the bottled salad dressings, I purchased inexpensive canola oil, red wine vinegar, and a tub of Dijon mustard, and I taught our volunteers how to make a simple vinaigrette that would work on almost any salad. It became clear that my elevated food skills as a chef were enabling us to do better (more delicious) things with the humble ingredients we had to use. Cooking for this lunch service taught me that the food on a plate communicates the values and attitude of the kitchen that produced it. It was vital to me that our message was clear: everyone has intrinsic value and deserves to not just survive but thrive. "When we place value on people by putting a little more time, money, and thought into them — really caring for them — the impact is exponential," said Sarah Watson, the director of community engagement for North York Harvest Food Bank in Toronto and a former Stop co-worker. I saw the truth of this every day at The Stop; just a little more care in how food was cooked and a small investment to get more fresh, wholesome ingredients on those plates made a huge impact in our ability to redefine a drop-in lunch menu and help change outcomes for our community. I didn't want to serve reheated frozen food, or highly processed food from a can, and was committed to doing the extra work to produce simple meals, all from scratch. But there's more to it than just the food on the plates. It's the fact that people get served at their table for lunch and that everyone is welcomed into the space by kind and friendly staff and volunteers. For me, this is about a fierce commitment to both delivering hospitality and maintaining dignity.

The Good Food for All Festival from the top of this chapter really brought home this lesson too. This event was started as an annual harvest festival hosted by The Stop, as a celebration of our community and our programs. Usually the food for community events like these looks a lot like the lunches served during regular programming, and guests line up to get themselves a bowl of soup or chili with a hunk of bread and some salad. This is a fine offering, but I wanted to make something more celebratory for this special occasion and decided instead that we would do passed hors d'oeuvres. The menu was simple but made with good ingredients that celebrated our harvest, and it was served with some style and elegance. My plan was to have our volunteers walk around with trays of food, and I even washed aprons and sourced compostable cocktail napkins for them to really look the part of serving staff. The trays were the same well-used aluminium ones we cooked on every day, but this time they held lovely little mouthfuls and a tent card with a description of the dish. The hours before a big event like this are always a bit chaotic, and amidst all of it, I found myself teaching volunteers how to steadily hold a tray and use a fist to make that impressive swirl of cocktail napkins so that each one is easy for guests to pick up. I remember shaking my head at myself for always choosing the more complicated option without having the human resources to pull it off. But when one of the volunteers came back into the kitchen with an empty tray and the biggest smile on her face, I knew that it had been worth the effort. I worked overtime assembling trays to keep up with the demand. Community members would pop their heads into the kitchen to tell us how good the food was and what a nice surprise the fancy canapés were. These were people who may have never found themselves at events with waitstaff passing around trays of hors d'oeuvres, and I was delighted to be able to offer them the chance to be served and pampered.

At the peak of intensity on this service, there was a knock on the kitchen door, and a young cook named Scott MacNeil poked his head in, offering his assistance. Scott had worked in a few kitchens in the city, was well versed in catering service, and ready to help. I couldn't believe that this most perfect person appeared to have fallen directly from the heavens into my kitchen, but I happily put him to work, handing him an apron and two shallow hotel pans of pear spice cake that needed to be portioned and topped with a hit of mascarpone cream. Scott spent the rest of the afternoon in the kitchen with me, building beautiful trays of passed apps and being the most incredible and instant support. The following summer, we hired Scott to support our growing kitchen programming, and that following spring, I left The Stop, placing the reins of the kitchen into Scott's very capable hands. He went on to run that kitchen for almost 10 years, refining the model and serving the community some of the most wholesome, delicious food that kitchen has ever produced. Scott and I remain dear friends and colleagues, often recalling that sunny September afternoon when he just showed up at the door and offered to help. In addition to making everything easier, Scott's arrival signalled to me that what I was doing in that kitchen was something compelling and that other chefs were interested in it. I remember driving home that day fully exhausted with sore feet and a joyful heart bursting with gratitude that we had actually pulled this thing off.

Each year, The Stop has a gala fundraiser that generates a large portion of their annual budget to support staffing and programming. The Stop is lucky to have an incredibly generous community of chefs and producers who donate product and time to support our vital programs. One year, half of a naturally raised cow was donated for the live auction at this event. To our delight, the person who had been the successful bidder on that cow then promptly donated the meat to the kitchen. I had the joyful task of deciding how the meat would be butchered, and which cuts we would use. Scott suggested that we keep the hip intact and roast it for the annual general meeting, which was the one time each year we had community members, staff, volunteers, and board members together for a dinner. We rubbed the roast with garlic and herbs, then roasted it overnight and slowly reduced a beef stock into a rich, luxurious demi-glace to be the sauce. The kitchen smelled wonderful all day, and I could not have been prouder to wheel that big hip of beef into the dining room. Naturally raised meat was not something that we were able to afford to serve our community members, and it was a real treat to carve this meat tableside with all of the pomp and circumstance that we could muster. I think that one of the best things about being a chef in a community food context is the opportunity to offer experiences like this to community members. For a variety of reasons (poverty, hospitalization, etc.), these folks don't find themselves in situations where there's a hip of beef being carved for dinner. They don't have the opportunity to be served, and desperation or insecurity has removed the celebration and pleasure from their relationship with food. Kindness, good service, and hospitality should not be things with a price tag but essential values of any kitchen and dining room.

Nothing really makes me happier than learning some recipes with a bunch of interested people in the kitchen. During my time at The Stop, I ran the community kitchens program, which offers community members the chance to connect with each other while cooking some food and to enjoy the fruits of that shared labour with a meal and often a little something to take home as well. One of the most popular community kitchen sessions we did was when I showed the group how to make their own chicken wings that were just as delicious as restaurant wings (and a fraction of the cost). I remember everyone's faces when we pulled the wings out of the oven, eyes wide with delight. "They look just like in the restaurant!" someone exclaimed, others nodding their heads in enthusiastic agreement. The wings were devoured in no time, and recipes went home so people could recreate them for their friends and family. That session was a lesson for me too: once again I was reminded of how a chef's skills could close the knowledge gap and put access to good, delicious food in people's hands.

Stop community members are surveyed annually for their feedback on services and programs and about the impact their participation in our programs is having on their lives (and their food security). What we learned from these surveys is that serving and distributing food is not actually the most valuable thing about our programming. We learned that reducing social isolation and creating the opportunity for people to come out of their homes to connect with other people is what matters most. Community food security is about more than just meeting basic needs. It's about connecting and sharing with others while also nourishing yourself. As humans, food is our common denominator — it's the vehicle that brings us to the garden, the kitchen, and the table. And as we participate in growing, cooking, and sharing food, our bodies are nourished, but so are our spirits. These are the moments when we can see people's experiences start to shift from simply surviving to actually thriving.

We had an 800-square-foot organic garden that the urban agriculture team tended lovingly, and each season, this garden would generate hundreds of pounds of beautiful organic produce to be shared between the kitchen and the food bank. During the growing season, I would get harvests from the garden two to three times a week, and the garden staff would leave me nice notes about what was in the fridge. It was there that I grew a deep respect for what was coming out of the earth and making its way into my kitchen. Bags of peppers, eggplants, zucchinis, and cucumbers would greet me in the morning, as well as fresh herbs and pig weed, a bitter green leafy vegetable that our community members from the Caribbean instantly identified as their beloved callaloo. In recent years, The Stop has developed the Global Roots gardens, an urban agriculture program focused on growing food from other climates and cultures, making local food also culturally appropriate and creating space for community members to learn about growing organic food from around the world.

One afternoon, one of the garden staff came into the kitchen and handed me round berries sheathed in a paper husk. She smiled at me and said, "They're ground cherries, try one!" I pulled off the wrapping and popped the yellow-orange berry into my mouth. It had the bright tartness of a gooseberry but finished with an almost mysterious hazelnut richness. These little treats that come with a harvest offering just enough to share with the folks who work in the garden provide experiences that cannot be bought from a grocery store. I made sure that I used every mouthful of that garden produce in our programs. It felt like a special wealth to me: this was our ideal food! It was organic produce, grown a couple of blocks away by a group of staff and volunteers who all share in the labour and harvest . . . and it tasted really good! *This* was the food everyone should be eating, and while we couldn't afford to buy it to serve to community members, we could grow it. There were days when I'd see generous bagfuls of organic tomatoes packed up for the food bank and piles of zucchini waiting to be taken home by the mothers in our perinatal program. Moments like these showed me that we really were making an impact on people's lives.

According to a 2008 paper in the *Cambridge Journal of Regions, Economy and Society*, "Garden programs provided opportunities for constructive activities, contributions to the community, relationship and interpersonal skill development, informal social control, exploring cognitive and behavioral competence, and improved nutrition. Community gardens promoted developmental assets for involved youth while improving their access to and consumption of healthy foods."

Another late summer afternoon, the urban agriculture team rolled in a wheelbarrow full of tomatillos. These tomato-like beauties are a member of the gooseberry family and have that distinctive paper husk around them. Inside the husk is a slightly slimy layer that needs to be washed off before you eat or cook with them, so they're a good bit of work to process. I decided that the best thing to do was to make jars of salsa verde that I could preserve and unlock in the deep of winter, when we were all in need of something fresh and green. I had a simple recipe, involving tomatillos, garlic, jalapeño, onion, a bit of lime, and some salt. At the time, many of The Stop's staff and volunteers were from Central and South America, and they all had their own opinions about how a salsa verde is supposed to taste. As I roasted tomatillos and chopped the ingredients for the salsa, staff members and volunteers from different Latin American countries walked through the kitchen, and I offered everyone a taste in exchange for their opinions about the flavour. What ensued was nothing short of hilarious: the Mexican wanted more heat, the Ecuadorian wanted more cilantro, and the Chilean thought it could be a bit sweeter. The final version was a sort of hybrid of all of this amazing input, and it remains one of the most collaborative recipes in The Stop's vast collection. What started as an exercise in managing a bumper crop turned into a charming process that connected people to a sense of home, culture, and tradition. We were putting our values on the plate and were slowly building our very own culture of food in the kitchen at The Stop.

In spring 2006, I received an invitation to participate in the first annual Picnic at the Brickworks, a combined fundraiser for Slow Food, an international food advocacy organization, and Evergreen, a national organization focused on preserving and promoting the importance of time spent in the natural environment. Jamie Kennedy, a treasured Canadian chef and pioneer of farm-to-table eating in Canada, sent us the invitation, and I was chuffed he knew who we were and thought we belonged in the lineup. This invitation told me that I was being considered on par with the other chefs in this city and that my operation was just as legit as any other, and that was *very* exciting. Unfortunately, this wasn't something that The Stop had ever done before. We didn't do big events, and we certainly hadn't ever donated our efforts towards someone else's fundraiser. But I really wanted to put The Stop's values into action and on display and to introduce us to the broader food community. We had a very important message to share about food, and the community of folks who would be at events like this would likely share our values around food, justice, and community. They were exactly the right people for us to speak to and, as participants at a high-end food event, great possible donors.

I wanted to tell everyone what we were doing at The Stop to improve and enrich the lives of our community members and, thankfully, I got my green light to participate. I arranged for all food ingredients to be donated and had only volunteer labour (including my own) involved in the prep. Stephen Alexander from Cumbrae's Meats donated some of his beautiful naturally raised beef for my dish, and I decided to do a beef vindaloo with cucumber yogurt, served on fresh little chapatis toasted on-site. But I needed 700 portions! The day before the event, things were going smoothly, but there was *a lot* to do, and I honestly wasn't sure if I was going to pull it off. Before I left for the day, I printed up a sign for my station that said, "This dish was prepared with 39 hours of volunteer labour, we hope you enjoy it!" If I couldn't pull this off, it felt important to communicate with people about what I was *trying* to do. I had colleagues Rhonda and Cheryl at the station helping me serve and talk about The Stop, and Glenn, my most loyal volunteer, toasting chapatis like a boss.

To my exhausted delight, we did it! The food turned out beautifully, people devoured it, and we got rave reviews. The most frequent questions we were asked were "Where can I come and eat this food?" and "What is The Stop?" It didn't feel quite right to invite these folks to our twice-weekly drop-in lunches, so more of a conversation was required to explain both The Stop and our mission. Moving forward, I made sure the food we served at events could be recognized by a community member as something they ate in one of our programs. It might be plated on china with a bit more style, but it was also something we regularly served for lunch. The Stop is ultimately a good news story, and having us there serving a crazy delicious dish and talking about the programs we've built to use good food to nurture our community got people's attention.

The post-Picnic media mentioned our station as a favourite, the fundraising team even saw a few donations come in, and there was a palpable excitement in the food community about what we were doing. I remember driving home from the event, exhausted but giddy at having been able to tell a really different and compelling story about community food security.

After our popular run at the Picnic at the Brickworks, word about The Stop and our successful foray into uncharted territory started to spread amongst the culinary community. I was so excited about it and wanted to share our approach with other chefs. Regardless of where we cook, on some level, chefs do what we do because of a love of feeding people. The Stop had me feeding seriously and often desperately hungry people, and there is a deep joy and satisfaction in doing so that is not often experienced in restaurants. I felt it from my first lunch service, and I knew that the moment any of my colleagues from restaurant kitchens came to cook with us, they'd feel it too.

I invited Jamie Kennedy to cook lunch with us one day and was thrilled when he took me up on the offer. Jamie brought a pork belly confit and some delicious white beans with him to serve for lunch. This was a much richer thing than I was ever able to serve, and it was nice to have this treat for our community members. The kitchen was at max capacity that day, full of volunteers who wanted to cook with our very famous guest chef. As usual, those three hours before service were busy and focused. At one moment, I looked up from cleaning greens from the garden to see Jamie searing pork belly on the flat top while checking on cornbread in the oven. The gorgeous rich smell of that belly hung in the air, and all of the staff and volunteers walking through commented on how they'd never smelled anything like this in our kitchen before. Naturally, Jamie was wearing chef's whites, a very normal visual in a restaurant kitchen but something quite out of the ordinary in a place like The Stop. I had intentionally decided not to wear chef's whites and opted instead for brightly coloured T-shirts with the same apron that volunteers wore, in the interest of minimizing any distance that could exist between me and the community I was serving. At the end of the meal, many community members came up to thank Jamie for the food and his visit. Almost all of them mentioned how thrilled they were to have a real chef cooking for them! I laughed and laughed and reminded these folks that they did, in fact, have a real chef cooking for them every day. But this was an important lesson to me: having someone like Jamie Kennedy come and cook lunch for them was a big deal. Being fed by a chef actually lifted some of our community members' sense of themselves. Happily, cooking lunch with us was also a big deal for Jamie. He was impressed by what we'd created at The Stop and grateful to have been able to feed truly hungry people.

I started working at The Stop at the end of 2005, and in 2006, Michael Pollan published *The Omnivore's Dilemma*, a grim articulation of the problematic state of our food system and its impact on our health and lives. Eric Schlosser had already opened eyes in 2001 with *Fast Food Nation*, his fast food industry exposé, and the team at The Stop had already been paying attention to the writing from revolutionary voices like Wendell Berry, Marion Nestle, and Wayne Roberts for decades. We often found ourselves talking about the problems with the current state of our food system and how our community members were often among the most negatively impacted. On the shelves of our food bank, I would see the many manifestations of corn that Michael Pollan talks about, and we would hear stories from community members who worked and still couldn't afford to feed their family.

As a social justice organization committed to increasing food security, The Stop was deeply involved in these issues on a local level. But how can you go against the dominant system with little to no resources? How can you be the change you want to see when you can't always make ends meet and put food on the table? And how can a small, well-intentioned community in the west end of Toronto do anything at all to help solve the global food crisis? These are the kinds of questions that would fill my head as I drove home from work and every time I'd drive to a discount grocery store to purchase ingredients for lunch. It was clear to me that local sourcing was a more sustainable way to do things, but at the time, there wasn't much local food available to us. And with our tiny budget, I often had to choose the most cost-effective import to feed the 200 folks who were expecting lunch. For folks who didn't eat every day, a focus on the origin of the food and how it was grown was unrealistic and a bit insulting. Let's secure a steady supply of real, perishable, albeit conventionally grown food to keep people alive, I told myself, then we can think about where it came from and how it was grown. We had a lot of distance to cover, but we weren't going to bridge that gap in one leap. Breaking things down into more manageable chunks allowed me first to focus on breaking away from industrial, packaged food and getting whole food onto the plates, then I could work on local sourcing and organic growing.

In the fall of 2008, I had an incredible opportunity to broaden my knowledge and perspective on these issues. Slow Food, an international organization focused on preserving, valuing, and maintaining the traditions of the farm and the table, was hosting an event in the San Francisco city centre to highlight some of the damaging issues in our food system, while also offering a living example of a more food-focused approach to community and civic life. The showpiece of this festival was a big victory garden in front of San Francisco city hall. There were native species, our beloved three sisters (squash, corn, and beans), huge cheerful sunflowers, and lovely signs everywhere telling stories about the plants. What really hit me were all of the examples of the better alternative, the new solution to the problem. There were food stalls serving the most delicious things, with signage about where the ingredients were sourced and how the food was prepared. It was the first time I had seen compostable disposables, and we were encouraged to only take what we needed. There were big compost piles with stories about turning the heap and the incredible work of a collection of worms. We ate our tacos on hay bales and chairs made from old magazines, and I was delighted to float around, taking photos of signage with sustainability messaging, making notes about games and activities I could use in programming, and learning about how to grow and share these good food values in my own work. The budding activist inside me really liked the idea of using our meal service as an act of resistance. In a world dominated by industrial food, capitalism, and income disparity, the fact that we could serve whole, honest, delicious food to all of our community members and evoke the tradition of the lunch table as a place for people to connect to each other and to good food felt radical.

One of the mandates of Slow Food is to preserve the traditions of the table, and tradition and history were becoming quite important to me as I continued to grow as a chef. I learned that by asking our community members for recipes and menu ideas, and then using them in our programming, I was able to bring some of that history and tradition alive for people and connect them to a different kind of wealth. It was very important to me that our menus reflected the cultural diversity of the community we served; I wanted people to see themselves on our plates and know that we saw them.

At Slow Food Nation, I heard Vandana Shiva speak for the first time. She's a quantum physicist and one of the loudest global voices against the proliferation of GMO agriculture and the commodification of life, as she describes it. She believes that small biodiverse farms are a more just way to treat the land that will more than adequately feed the planet. Plus, she's a fierce aunty who wears nice silk sarees and the world's biggest bindis. She knows exactly what she believes, and her ability to use fact and truth to skillfully knock down the line of critics and doubters that inevitably forms for the Q&A portion of her talks is jaw-dropping. I also sat in on a series of panels bursting with expert voices on a series of food issues. I remember marvelling at how much good food expertise was in one room at one time! One of the panels was like the Avengers of food, and we were treated to a conversation between Eric Schlosser, Michael Pollan, Alice Waters, Raj Patel, Vandana Shiva, Wendell Berry, *and* Carlo Petrini.

Since I was in San Francisco, I made a pilgrimage to Berkeley to Chez Panisse, Alice Waters's famous restaurant. Aside from being a chef, Waters is the vice chancellor for Slow Food International and the founder of the Edible Schoolyard Project, an innovative and holistic approach to education that is anchored in growing, cooking, and sharing food. As a young woman, Waters spent time in France and ate everything. The beautiful quality of food in France and the cultural importance that food played in daily life left an indelible imprint on her. She returned to the U.S. with so much conviction about introducing both these flavours and attitudes to Americans. Waters is credited with being the mother of the farm-to-table movement in the U.S. and is the reason why we have classic dishes like walnut crusted chèvre on mesculin greens. She may not have grassroots strategies for a community food centre, but she's someone who reminds us about the truth and power of good, pure food.

I took a group of friends with me to dinner at Chez Panisse. We sat at a table by the kitchen and felt the heat of the fire that was roasting squab and mushrooms for the entrée. Now, a full 10 years later, the simplicity and purity of the flavours is still with me: the sweetness of those figs with the char of the squab; the fresh, green flavour of the peach leaf ice cream; and the playful crunch of the cucumbers on the fish. In her hunt for the best, freshest produce she could get her hands on, Waters also shortened the supply chain and raised what farmers got paid for their work. And even though the business didn't actually turn a profit until more than 30 years in, Alice Waters and Chez Panisse taught us all that good, well-grown food is an anchor for a restaurant and kitchen. Everything comes down to the food. You stand on the quality of your ingredients, which good cooks know require very little to prepare. After dinner, I peeped into the kitchen at Chez Panisse and saw a lone young cook packing up the last few bits from service. I said hello and outed myself as a cook, wanting only to run my fingers over the large cutting board on the counter. This cook was quite kind and invited me to tour the fridges and look around. She knew what a big deal that kitchen was. Before I knew it, I was standing in the Chez Panisse vegetable fridge! Everything was recently harvested and distinctly fresh and alive. The crates of greens were even labelled with the first names of the farmers who grew them.

As though this wasn't enough inspiration, just a few short weeks after I returned home from Slow Food Nation in San Francisco, I got on a plane to Torino, Italy, for Terra Madre, a biennial global conference, put on by Slow Food. Every single person I had met who had been to Terra Madre told me that it was life changing. The original version of this conference focused primarily on farmers, or producers, and was created in the hopes of being the largest global collection of peasants. That community has since grown to include cooks, students, journalists, and media, but for many delegates, the journey from home started with a ride on an animal — these are people who work the land, not the usual sort to wear a conference ID badge around their neck.

Being in an arena full of people from around the world who were so deeply committed to making change was a huge, inspirational rush, and two major things struck me over the course of the five days at Terra Madre. First, I had found my people. These were people who were terrified about the future of our food system, who shared my values about preserving the culture and tradition of food in kitchens and on tables, and who were actively working and fighting for people to take food more seriously. And second, the impact of the corporatization of agriculture around the world is horribly dismal. Listening to the story of a Mexican corn farmer who has been pushed off his land will break your heart, and every producer I spoke to had some version of this grim tale to tell. My heart and my stomach ached after listening to the multitude of ways that people's lives had been destroyed by a profits-driven attitude to agriculture and food production. There were about 6,000 of us there, each tuned in with headsets, connected by smiles and some pretty deeply shared values. We told stories, we commiserated, we shared lessons and victories, and we ate lots of delicious food!

Italy is the land of so many mouth-watering things: I tasted honey infused with the earthiness of black truffles, ate fresh arancini from a gas station, and had a plate of pasta that made me weep. It doesn't matter how much you spend on the wine, it's all delicious. Why is Italian food so good? It's mostly because Italians take food *very* seriously. They are firmly anchored in tradition, with clear ideas about how you make a tomato sauce, what a real pizza tastes like, and how you should never put cheese on seafood pasta. Stopping for an espresso simply because it smelled so good is a legitimate reason to be late for a meeting, and Italians generally remain quite offended by cheap, low-quality food. Italy was one thing, but we were in a Slow Food bubble, especially at the Salone del Gusto, the most glorious food trade show I had ever seen. The San Daniele booth was lined with legs of their prosciutto, and a man worked the wheel of the slicer for hours on end, draping a ribbon of prosciutto over the outstretched fingers of people waiting patiently in line. I tasted olive oils that were soft and buttery, and others that burned the gutter of my mouth. I sampled fresh torrone, pistachio paste, and a farinata wrapped around the gooiest, most deliciously salty cheese. There were cabbage sandwiches doused heavily with garlic, anchovies, and olive oil; pasta stuffed with sticky braised meats; and confections that boasted the most glorious, real fruit flavour I had ever tasted. Terra Madre taught me that food was about the land and that there is an interconnected chain of hands involved in moving food from field to kitchen to table. It taught me that when I do something on one side of the planet, ripples of impact can be felt on the other side. It also reminded me that eating is about so much more than just consuming calories; there is joy, pleasure, and connection in sharing a meal with others at a table that is in just as much jeopardy as the food ingredients themselves.

I returned home bursting with knowledge and inspiration. I felt as though I had gone to drink from the source and was now tasked with keeping those good Slow Food vibes and values alive with my work. I remember standing in the kitchen at The Stop, trying to find ways in which I could bring the wisdom of these lessons to life in this space. What do Slow Food values look like in a community food centre? How do you prioritize paying producers fairly when you barely have any food budget? And what can I do as a chef to make sure that these values of good, clean, and fair food breathe throughout the way we grow, cook, and share food? Two important lessons emerged here. First, I was driven by the idea that as we work to rebuild the food system, it could not only exist for those who can afford it. The only truly sustainable version of our food system is one that includes everyone. Truthfully, this made the task a bit more complicated, which I could accept in the name of inclusion. And second, while we may not have had a lot of money to spend on food, we did have some, and I could still use these values of sustainability and justice to guide my purchasing decisions. I worked with our food bank coordinator to build relationships with local farmers. Though our budgets were lean, the one advantage we could offer local producers was a reliable volume purchase, which often earned us a bit of a discounted price. Sometimes we'd get a deal on some seconds or slightly misshapen produce. This process was slow, but it was effective, and we were able to use our modest food budget to nurture closer connections between producer and consumer while getting fresh, wholesome, local food into our programming.

Almost every recurring program The Stop had required some form of food. Many of the coordinators were shopping for their own program snacks, and it all felt a bit fragmented. I took over the task of purchasing and prepping the food for almost all of the programs. I felt the responsibility to support my co-workers, and that involved me taking the shopping off their plates so they could focus on their work. This also allowed me to consolidate purchasing, which is more efficient, and it also allowed me to use our values to guide our spending. When peaches were in season, I could reach out to a farmer to get a supply for all programs, and the volume allowed us to make a nicely sized order for the whole organization. When a donation of oats came in, I knew that two programs needed granola the following week and to save that for them.

In addition to this admin stuff, I wanted to improve the vibe in the physical space of the kitchen. It was important to me that the kitchen be as cheerful as possible. I bought a few big posters with bright, colourful images of local produce, and I found a few of my favourite quotes about food, printed them up, and posted them randomly around the kitchen. We bought a stereo, and volunteers would bring their own kitchen CD mixes in. We'd always listen to music while we were prepping lunch, and it would be so nice to see folks dance their way through the kitchen on those mornings, trying to figure out what was for lunch by what they were smelling. I realize now that these were my early experiments in building a culture of food anchored by the kitchen. The Stop began to feel different from other community kitchen spaces, which meant we were able to start asserting some of our own ideas about food and cooking.

Food at The Stop was both a resource and a tool, and we understood the incredible opportunity we had to connect a good food conversation to ideas of justice, equity, and diversity. We served wholesome, delicious breakfasts and lunches to our community, but we also made sandwiches for a protest march at Queen's Park. I did cooking demos during the farmers' market and also gave a deputation at City Hall about the importance of investing in a municipal food strategy. Food is never just food. It was very important to me that our organizational values be present on every plate, but even articulating those values was a long road.

People talk a lot about the importance of serving healthy food, and while I instinctively agree with this, I have a few questions: What does "healthy" mean? Who decides what healthy food is? Does everyone have the freedom to choose healthy food for themselves? And however well-meaning our intentions, it would be very easy for us to slide into the role of paternalistic, finger-wagging "health" authority that comes with so much of this kind of institutionalized food service. Slow Food had shown me the importance of local, seasonal eating, and so I used those values about good food and sustainability in meal planning and preparation. Also, we had other values that needed to be included: securing access to food that was appropriate for people's cultural/dietary needs, supporting farmers, and making sure eating could once again be joyful and full of great flavour. Finally I came up with the first tag line I ever used for my food: wholesome, affordable, and delicious. These three words provided a quick, easy way to vet menus and recipes for programming.

In 2009, The Stop published a cookbook, *Good Food for All*, which demonstrates those values on every page. It's a book full of fresh, seasonal recipes and stories about The Stop, its programs, and its community members. This was a cookbook embraced by food lovers that sold speedily at our local independent grocer, and every single one of those recipes was served during programming. The people who bought heirloom tomatoes and the first ramps of the season would be eating the same thing as those in our community kitchens, who I fed for a mere $1.85 a plate. And everyone would be eating *well*. The cookbook allowed me to share some of my chef's knowledge and made it clear that good food wasn't a frill — it was a foundation.

At The Stop, the kitchen really became the heart of the organization. Physically, it was a thoroughfare that connected office and programming spaces, but we also built a culture that prioritized food and community in a way that offered an emotional connection to other people as well. Alice Waters once said that "the kitchen is a place where you can find something inside of you that you did not know was there," and I watched striking discoveries and transformations on the regular. I've seen how preparing salads for lunch can make people with a workplace injury feel useful and productive. I've watched a known community thug squeal with delight as he tasted the fluffy buttercream frosting he'd made for a cake. I've had belly-bursting laughs with non-verbal volunteers during an heirloom vegetable tasting, and I've seen the task of prepping lunch turn a group of otherwise boisterous, rowdy teenage boys into a productive, efficient team. The kitchen allowed people to shed old self-perceptions and limitations and see themselves in a new context.

That transformation happened to me too. My almost five years at The Stop was an incredible source of knowledge and education. I was delighted to see how my skills and training helped to augment the food we served and the programming we offered, and I was so inspired by the incredible future possibilities I saw for chefs and communities. The kitchen at The Stop was the place where my love for food and feeding people blossomed. I also got really lucky and had the most incredible team of co-workers who made the work joyful and the hard days bearable. These folks were smart, committed, generous, and capable, and I still have close relationships with so many of them today. I got to experiment with ways to be a chef in a non-profit kitchen, and I had both the responsibility and opportunity to walk my talk and show up for our community with good food. For me, it was a perfect fit.

Nine years after leaving my job at The Stop, I was back in that kitchen as a board member, helping the team cook a winter solstice brunch. The incredibly talented and committed Monica Bettson is the chef at the helm, and her food is thoughtful and delicious. When I walked into the kitchen, Monica had cranberry brioche sweet buns just out of the oven, volunteers traying up artisanal bacon, and others putting together a smoked salmon cream cheese for the baked Mennonite eggs. We topped this meal off with fluffy oat pancakes that got generously doused with real maple syrup. This food was all purchased from a local supplier. We were able to get these beautiful ingredients into the kitchen in a way that didn't require the producer to offer a discount or a charitable consideration. Everyone along this chain was paid fairly, and the glory of the situation is that The Stop's incredible team has been able to both enjoy incredibly innovative purchasing relationships with local producers, such as The New Farm, and raise enough money to afford food from local farms and suppliers. It's a diversified approach through connections that allow everyone to get paid and fed well.

As I prepped pans for the eggs, I thought about all of the lunches that I had cooked in that kitchen over the course of my five years at The Stop. I had spent a lot of time torn between the dream of the food I wanted to serve (which is also the food that this very vulnerable community *should* be eating) and the food I was actually able to serve, with a very minimal budget. That winter solstice brunch menu was all food I had only dreamed of being able to serve our community. I wanted everyone to taste the deliciousness of good, well-raised food, to be able to cook things with cream, and indulge in lovely things like real maple syrup instead of some corn syrup–based substitute. And most of all, I wanted to be able to make it work. I wanted to serve good food in a way that preserved people's dignity and nurtured their well-being. And our organizational values wanted us to pay people fairly for their work. In the effort to rebuild our food system, we have to be very careful not to build something and call it a success if it only exists for those who can afford it. A place that started as a food bank in a church basement has grown into an international example for community food-security programming and advocacy. It has grown from offering handouts of canned food to a solstice brunch that any hipster would line up for. This work is both complex and challenging, but when everyone involved buys into a new vision, so much change is possible. This is a total institutional transformation — yes, on a small scale but pulled off with extremely limited resources. Even in the non-profit world, even in overlooked and disenfranchised communities, food can have a seat at the table.

CHAPTER 3

HOSPITALS

Putting the Hospitality Back into Hospital Food

"We've got a health care system that doesn't care about food, and a food system that doesn't care about health."
— WENDELL BERRY, FARMER AND AUTHOR

Picture it: it's 1980, and you've just woken up from surgery. You're a bit achy and dopey, and once you've spent a bit of time with your eyes open, you get a message from your stomach. You're hungry. You've been hungry since yesterday, and now you need something to eat. The smell of cooking wafts through the hallway as lunch trays get delivered to patients. A friendly face enters your room and places a tray in front of you, and as soon as that dome gets lifted, the first thing that hits you is the smell of a toasty fresh roll, still warm from the oven. The roll is soft, and the perfect thing to dip into the rich gravy of a beef stew, which sits atop a pile of fragrant, fluffy rice. The beef in that stew was butchered on-site, and the stew was made with a beef broth that simmered in a kettle for hours to achieve maximum flavour and nutrition. Beside the stew there are crisp, lemony green beans and a fresh tomato salad. A small bowl holds a piece of apple cake topped with a little hit of custard, and later this afternoon someone will come by offering tea or coffee. You're moving slowly, but you cannot resist the urge to start eating. The food is simple and seasoned and portioned conservatively. But it is real, made from whole ingredients, and, perhaps most importantly, tastes good. There is life in the food, and once you place your fork down on an empty plate, you feel full and restored.

Now, let's fast-forward 32 years to 2012: I'm visiting a hospital in Toronto that has just invested hundreds of thousands of dollars on new retherm units, used to heat up patient meals. We enter one room with tiled walls and about 15 electric plugs on cords, evenly spaced out, hanging from the ceiling. I ask if this room is still under construction, but no — this is a finished space, where the retherm boxes get plugged in to do their job. This isn't the beginning of something, this is the end of it.

My tour continues through a labyrinth of cold hallways, each heavy, industrial door opening to a walk-in fridge or freezer the size of an average family kitchen. In here, staff work with winter gear on, their hands in fingerless gloves that get covered by disposable gloves, to plate up patient meals. If all this feels dystopian, that's because it is.

Let's take a minute to review what that meal from 1980 looks like now: that beef stew is prepared somewhere off-site, portioned, and frozen into pucks. Same thing with the rice. And the gravy on the stew is so full of powdered base and cornstarch that you're likely not that interested in mopping any of it up with your bun, which has one pretty flat texture, no crusty outside, and minimal flavour. It is also made elsewhere and frozen, and then brought back to life in a steamer or oven. The tomato salad arrives with a foil seal and a bunch of preservatives to keep it shelf stable. Dessert is some kind of apple cake that is baked off-site, portioned into a cup, frozen, and then thawed out — or mostly thawed, because you inevitably find an icy core. There's certainly no custard. There's a lukewarm cup of tea or coffee already on your tray and a cup of water, again sealed with foil.

Beyond the flavour and textural differences, you can tell that one of these two meals is made just a few floors below you, and the other is distinctly from somewhere else — nobody has any information about where, it all just arrived in a cardboard box on a skid a couple of days ago.

If patient trays reflect the values of the institution serving them, what does this plummeting service standard tell vulnerable folks in hospital? That ease and affordability are more important than their health and dignity. The average patient stay in Ontario is four to six days, so patients get told a minimum of 12 times during their stay in the hospital that they're not worth any more effort than that miserable tray of industrial, processed, overpackaged food.

So how did we get from freshly baked rolls to frozen pucks of stew? I'll focus on Ontario, which is where I do most of my work, but you'll see similar themes and patterns elsewhere. From 1995 to 2002, Ontario's Progressive Conservative Party, led by Mike Harris, implemented what they called a "Common Sense Revolution." In an attempt to reduce the provincial deficit and personal income tax rates, the Harris Conservatives slashed and burned budgets, notably in health care, education, and social services. These short-sighted austerity measures are familiar moves from the government playbook. The health care sector was not told specifically where the cuts should happen, and because food in hospitals is considered little more than an irritating necessity, food and nutrition services budgets took some of the biggest hits. We started letting accountants make decisions about how we feed patients, often forcing nutrition staff to accept a standard of food that was "nutritionally adequate" for patients and tossing aside any notion of food's therapeutic role in patient care. We also decided that paying a human to prepare fresh food in hospitals was inefficient and expensive — most kitchens lost some staff, and some hospitals completely outsourced their food service to a third-party operator.

When things still needed to get leaner and meaner, snacks were taken off the menus or portions were reduced. Menu cycles were pared back, offering less choice and variety. Canada Bread was asked to squeeze 14 slices out of a loaf instead of 12, and the three-cent packet of Mrs. Dash, a sodium-free seasoning, was removed from trays. It is fair to say that scratch cooking patient meals is a thing of the past in the vast majority of hospitals and long-term care facilities in the country today.

The budgets for both labour and ingredients have been hollowed out, with help from the industrial food system. Some administrators continue to think there is fat to trim from food service budgets, but the truth is there is little to no fat on those menus anymore. Any budget cuts will mean scraping bone.

One day in 2011, I got an email from Paul DeCampo, a dear friend and colleague who was on the steering committee at Slow Food Toronto. He told me that they had received a request from a hospital in Scarborough that wanted to make some changes to their food service and were looking for some support and guidance. The folks at The Scarborough Hospital wanted to improve the patient experience and smartly realized that food was a big part of that. In fact, a brief by HealthCare*CAN* and the McConnell Foundation on the state of hospital food in Canada reported that "patients were four times as likely to rate their whole hospital stay with a perfect score when their rating of the food was excellent." Basically, the more patients like the food, the better they feel about their whole stay. I've chatted with some hospital administrators who tell me that the patients rate their food on the low end of satisfied. (Keep in mind: these surveys are usually given at discharge, when you'll say anything to get out of there and don't see any immediate benefit from negative feedback. What if we offered surveys on day two or three?) And while these scores highlight a big opportunity to do things differently, they're also (if you can believe it) not bad enough to really motivate much change. I even heard one hospital administrator say, "If they're well enough to complain about the food, they're well enough to go home."

Needless to say, I was excited to hear about a hospital that was looking to improve the patient experience and I jumped at the opportunity and met with Anne-Marie Males, then vice president of patient experience, and Susan Bull, the director of nutrition services. Both of these women were full of ideas and questions about how I could help them elevate the patient food experience. What was scheduled for a 90-minute meeting ended up lasting about three hours, and we were all bursting with excited possibility at the end of it. Fortunately for us, there was some newly available grant money via the provincial Greenbelt Fund to put more local food into public sector institutions. This grant money could pay for a consultant to manage the project, training for staff, and new equipment for the kitchen. Although the focus was on local food, I took this rare opportunity to jam my foot in the door and talk about other aspects of the food service too, like scratch cooking and more cultural diversity on the menus.

In my first days at the hospital, I spent a lot of time observing the operation. While the space may have looked like any other kitchen, with tiled walls, stainless steel counters, and walk-in fridges, it functioned in a very different way. For instance, there were no knives, oil, or salt. Not much is cooked without these three things. No knives meant that no raw ingredients were being broken down. The vast majority of produce was already chopped and frozen, and when staff started prepping meals, they would put on a parka and pull frozen bags of whatever they needed from the walk-in. No oil meant that the meals were not being built on a base of sautéed aromatics. Nothing was being browned — there was no conscious building of flavour happening here at all. Frozen ingredients were combined in a giant soup kettle and simply warmed up for service. And finally, the absence of salt shouldn't have been too much of a surprise in a health care context; meals were all intended to be low sodium. But no salt in the kitchen told me two things: there was no focus on flavour and the processed food that was being served already contained enough sodium, usually as a preservative. As long as the nutritional data was where it needed to be, that was enough. The whole did not need to be any greater than the sum of the parts.

Another important indicator of the kind of meal prep that was happening were the large white bins under the counters. Usually these would hold things that you have in big quantities, like grains and sugar, but beside the bin of all-purpose flour was a matching bin of cornstarch. I gasped when I saw this and wondered what was happening in this kitchen that required so much cornstarch. Cornstarch is primarily a thickener, but when you're cooking from scratch, it isn't usually required. Aromatics like onions, garlic, and celery are sautéed to build a flavourful base for a dish, and sometimes things like tomato purée, cream, and fortified stock are added to build sauces in the pan, which come together to give the food body. The flavours and textures of the dish are developed on a foundation of fresh ingredients. But with food that's been previously processed and frozen, the high water content from freezing makes it wet and spongy, leaving any body and fibre virtually undetectable. Thus, a cornstarch slurry is used to prop the food back up. It's *Weekend at Bernie's* cooking, and it hurts my heart.

The majority of the cooks in the kitchen at The Scarborough Hospital had been there for at least 10 or 15 years, many of them for 25 years or longer. The team remembered a time when that kitchen buzzed with activity, when they baked fresh rolls every morning and five full-time cooks prepared just vegetables. Sides of meat once hung in the walk-in fridge, and giant stockpots simmered all day instead of serving as expensive containers for large tools. Someone from the team dug up an old box containing the recipes that were once used to feed patients and presented it proudly to me one afternoon. The cards were appropriately yellowed, and the recipes told a story of a previous time: beef stroganoff, strawberry mousse, and Salisbury steak. Once again, the message was clear: I wasn't introducing new ideas, I was revisiting old ones.

But this, of course, isn't how food is made anymore. Generally speaking, there are three styles of food service in hospitals. First, the traditional model, which is what happened at The Scarborough Hospital, has food produced on-site each day. In most cases, this started out as scratch cooking, but currently it's a model that uses highly processed foods: vegetables that are chopped and frozen, meat that is cooked and frozen, stock and sauces made from a reconstituted powder base, and desserts that largely come from cans. All of these "shortcuts" have resulted in a lower labour requirement, as the chopping, seasoning, and flavour building have been eliminated from the process.

A second option is called the retherm model. Food is prepped, cooked, and frozen off-site, and staff wear parkas as they assemble trays in freezers, like at the hospital I visited. These trays go into a stainless steel box on wheels that has one hot side and one cold side, and they're plugged in until they reach the required minimum temperature for service, then rolled up to patient rooms and distributed. An ineffective seal between the two temperatures means patients often received warm milk and limp salad greens. At one hospital, they received so many patient complaints about limp salad greens, their solution was to just remove salad from the menu. The salad was easily the only fresh, unprocessed thing on the tray, but convenience won out over patient care.

The third model involves outsourcing food service to a third-party operator, which could mean one of these two options, or a third custom model. Operators are popular because they make the money work and take over the full breadth of patient feeding, including therapeutic diets, such as those for people with diabetic, cardiac, renal, or dental issues. Of course, this hassle-free model also comes with a serious downside: outsourcing food means outsourcing part of patient care to a profit-driven corporation.

As I observed The Scarborough Hospital kitchen, I discovered something else pretty quickly: much of the food that was sent up to patients came right back down to the kitchen and went straight into the trash. I watched carts of trays come back, many of them looking much the way they did when they left, and staff scraped everything into a garbage can. That's right, *everything*. There was no organic separation, no recycling or repurposing of anything. Whole bananas and oranges, whole cartons of milk, and cans of nutritional supplements would all get thrown away because the hospital's infection control mandate dictated nothing could be reused and that handling of returned food be kept to a minimum. In many instances, hospitals don't have organic waste separation or a proper system for recycling. While I understand the infection control concern, from an environmental perspective this is appalling, given all the energy and resources used to grow, package, and ship that food to the hospital in the first place. And this level of waste is by no means unusual: a meta-analysis in the journal *Clinical Nutrition* concluded between 6 and 65 percent of food served to patients is destined for the trash. A survey by Value Chain International suggests that Toronto hospitals waste more than a tonne of food per day, at a cost of

$1.50 per patient, per day. My mind is full of ideas about how we could use that money to buy better ingredients!

But beyond wasted money and squandered natural resources, here's the most important lesson: returned trays mean that patients aren't eating, and if they're not eating, they can't heal. In palliative care, one of the clearest indicators that the end of life is near is when a person stops eating. If nothing else, this serves as a sharp reminder that food and eating are about being and staying alive. The Canadian Malnutrition Task Force (CMTF) reports that about 45 percent of patients are malnourished when they arrive in hospital, and that "malnourishment is a predictor of a prolonged length of stay in the hospital." Another study from the same task force reports that "malnourished patients are at a higher risk of readmission into the hospital in 30 days." Janice Sorenson, a dietician and researcher with the CMTF, drove it home when she reminded me, "Food is only healthy if it's eaten." In her work, Janice focuses on hospital food being appetizing for patients. "The more patients eat, the stronger they get, the more ready they are to go home," she told me. Even the most penny-pinching taxpayer should see malnutrition is costing us, and what we don't spend on good food we're likely spending on longer hospital stays. (Remember, $842 per day!) Prioritizing patient care also allows us to turn the beds over as quickly as possible and make sure people aren't being treated in hallways or left waiting for care. Restoring a patient's health and well-being as quickly as possible is good for both the patient and the hospital. Like me, Janice believes that before anything else, hospital food needs to be appetizing and prepared more thoughtfully to "make every spoonful count." In the spirit of focusing on appetizing food, she wants to open up a space for chefs to play and experiment with ways to get more food into bellies. If food helps patients heal, then it makes perfect sense that it should be as inviting *and* nourishing as possible.

That said, some of our ideals around healthy eating do not work for people who are not well. A kale salad might not work for you after you've had chemotherapy or surgery or chronic illness. Sometimes we need to set aside Canada's Food Guide and offer patients comfort and appease their appetites. As much as I'm not a fan of high-fructose corn syrup, for a patient whose mouth is dry and taste buds have been hijacked by a medication, sometimes the most perfect thing is an ice cold Coke. Of course, I'm not suggesting that a patient *only* be fed Coke, but that it can be complemented by wholesome, nourishing food.

Something else that comes up a lot in complaints about hospital food is that mealtimes are easily missed. Patients get pulled for doctor's appointments, lab work, or other therapeutic care during mealtimes, which often results in them not getting to eat. The CMTF surveyed hospital patients in 2015 and uncovered 23 barriers to food intake. Some of these barriers are organizational, such as being pulled away for appointments, but other barriers have to do with the food service itself. Twenty-seven percent of patients reported being in an uncomfortable position to eat, and 30 percent of patients reported having difficulty opening packets and unwrapping food. This difficulty unwrapping food is especially important in a facility that relies heavily on packaged foods. I visited one hospital that had recently started purchasing sandwiches (remember that egg salad?) that were injected with an extra dose of CO_2 to keep them "fresh" in the fridge for seven days. To keep this extra gas inside that plastic triangle, the seal had to be reinforced with a stronger adhesive, and many patients were too weak to break through that reinforced seal. What good is your super "fresh" sandwich if nobody can actually eat it?

Right now, hospital food is generally prepared in the basement, alongside departments like laundry and janitorial services. Having the kitchen in the basement keeps food preparation isolated from patients. At one hospital that uses the travelling retherm model for patient meals, one of the most persistent patient complaints about this meal service was that the soup was always sloshed all over the tray due to the distance the retherm box had to travel to get from the kitchen to patient rooms. Important note: soup that's spilled all over a tray won't get eaten. If food is, in fact, considered an essential component to healing and restoring wellness, patients should experience more of it.

With exceptions for those whose medical circumstances make them sensitive to smell, in an ideal world, hospital patients would be able to smell their meals being prepared. Just like in any house, the smell of browning onions or baking bread or roasting vegetables wafts through the air as a signal to everyone that something good is happening in the kitchen. It's an encouraging indicator that someone is preparing something delicious for you.

What if muffins and breads got baked in kitchenettes among patient rooms? What if patients could smell a stew, slowly bubbling away for their dinner? Menu swaps and local greens are wonderful, but there's so much more we can do to put the health and humanity back in hospital food.

So, how do you rebuild a menu with all this in mind and with no extra resources for things like labour and ingredients? While nobody is willing to invest in food service — in fact, it's more likely that hospitals are working to implement yet another 2 to 3 percent budget shave — there are a few very creative people making innovative changes within the system. In my time doing this work, I've visited a number of institutional kitchens, and each time I'm there, I pay close attention to how the staff are getting meals prepped and out for service. The first kitchen I ever visited was Leslie Carson's at a long-term care facility in Guelph, Ontario, in 2011. I was told that Leslie was doing some incredible things with local ingredients and naturally raised meats, and I had to see it for myself. The service model Leslie was using was retherm, where food arrives cooked, portioned, and frozen, and staff plate up cold trays that are then stacked up in hot boxes, brought up to temperature, and wheeled out to patient rooms. Generally, the kitchens that put these trays together lack the familiar cooking appliances; I've walked past various sizes of steam and soup kettles, stoves, and ovens now lying dormant, running my finger through some dust and peeking through plastic, quietly apologizing to them all for this lousy existence. Over the course of the last few decades, fridges and freezers have become the workhorses in institutional kitchens, but dusty appliances are evidence that cooking could be revived.

Though she was stuck with the retherm system, Leslie had managed to wrangle herself a small double electric-coil burner that had the look of a well-worn machine that was working hard, with the numbers on the control dials long rubbed off and little burn marks outside the heated coil. On the day I visited, she was making a beef stew. She had some really nice pasture-raised beef from a local farm, and in a very large saucepot on one of the burners she had fresh aromatics like onions, celery, garlic, and herbs sautéing away to soften. She portioned out the chopped stewing beef into metal pans that also fit in the retherm units and topped the beef with those very familiar frozen discs of carrot, and she then ladled over this lovely sautéed aromatic mixture. A bit of beef broth and a stir, and these pans were covered and placed in the retherm units that Leslie was essentially using as low ovens to braise the meat. Wet carrots aren't such a problem in a stew, and this was a wonderful way to combine fresh and frozen. A couple of hours later, it looked and smelled totally delicious. The meat was tender, the sauce was rich, and that stew had become something greater than the sum of its parts.

I was impressed and inspired by Leslie's innovative, creative thinking and deep commitment to figuring it out. If you've got a steady source of low heat, then build a menu around that. Her idea of making a large quantity of an aromatic base, then portioning it out into the service pans provided so much great flavour for that dish. The meal was a hit at lunch, and when I peeked into the dining room, I realized how perfect this soft, braised food was for patients in long-term care, as so many of them are older people with dental and swallowing challenges. Leslie really reminded me that the only way to actually make any change was to figure out what I could do with what I had available to me and go from there.

The lead cook at The Scarborough Hospital was Debbie Lennox, who guides a very small team of people responsible for preparing meals for 324 patients. Debbie had worked in the hospital kitchen since she was 16 years old and is nothing short of a powerhouse, with a deep commitment to doing right by the patients in the beds upstairs. She has a bright, happy face and is proud of the great work she does. Like many of the other folks in the hospital kitchen, she has seen the food standards plummet, yet Debbie is still a model cook and the first one in the kitchen each morning. If she could deliver trays to every patient herself and sit with folks as they ate, she would. Debbie was my greatest ally in change-making, and I realized quickly that her input and involvement in rebuilding the regular patient menu was crucial.

We started by testing new recipes every Wednesday. We wanted recipes that were affordable, seasonal, scratch-made with locally sourced ingredients, delicious, culturally diverse, and easy to prepare — basically the stuff of a reality TV challenge. The first recipe we developed was for a carrot muffin. I wanted to create a base recipe for a muffin, using local whole grains, eggs, and dairy. Each season we could switch out chopped or grated fresh fruits and vegetables to this base. As we workshopped the recipe, we'd bake a batch, then taste them, evaluating the flavour, the batter-to-filling ratio, and the slope of the tops of the muffins, which told a story about how evenly (or not) the heat is distributed in the oven. When you're just warming up frozen things, you don't require your oven to do more than generate heat. But when you need to bake things, the performance of the equipment matters much more.

After two or three batch trials, we figured out the sourcing, flavour, texture, and cooking process on a new recipe, and the next step was to write it out, do the nutritional analysis online, and then submit it to the dietician team for their assessment. This is where things really got interesting. A UN-style negotiation inevitably occurred over salt and fat. I wouldn't compromise on flavour, and they wouldn't compromise on the need to meet the appropriate servings of salt, fat, and carbs for patients.

For example, I wanted to put a red fife biscuit on the menu. These hearty biscuits could be prepared ahead of time, frozen, then baked as needed to provide maximum flakiness. It was a nice, easy way for us to be able to produce fresh baked goods. I, of course, wanted to use real butter — a full-cream thing sourced from a local dairy — and the dietician team kept asking if I could make these biscuits with vegetable oil or margarine.

Let me just pause here to talk about butter and margarine. Dietetic culture in the 1980s did a marvellous job of making us all scared of fat, particularly saturated fat from an animal source. Butter, cream, marbled beef, chicken skin, and bacon were all placed irrevocably on the "bad for you" list of foods, and we filled our diets with things like boneless, skinless chicken breast, turkey bacon, and margarine. People ran from the rich, saturated, supposedly artery-clogging glory of butter, right into the arms of margarine, in all of its polyunsaturated, whipped vegetable oil glory. Not only was margarine considered better for your health, it also remained spreadable when refrigerated, an added benefit for food service, which served individual packets of margarine on patient trays. Ultimately, it was uncovered that the trans fats in margarine actually raised levels of bad cholesterol and suppressed levels of good cholesterol, which left margarine consumers feeling duped and prompted change and reformulation from industry.

My conversations with the dietician team about butter and margarine were the basis of my crystal-clear understanding that we had very different priorities about food. They were happy with the boxes unhydrogenated (non-trans fat) margarine ticked whereas I preferred the flavour of butter. I had some major issues with all of the ingredients and processes required to stabilize, colour, and whip margarine into its spreadable, soft, butter-like appearance, and I was vindicated just a few years later in 2017, when a team of British cardiologists confirmed that this long-standing vilification of saturated fat as an artery-clogging cause of heart disease was "just plain wrong." In moderation, a bit of butter is just fine, friends. Health and flavour aside, there's the food chemistry to consider: in an oven, butter melts in a way that creates little pockets of steam between layers of dough to make flakes in pastry. This simply doesn't happen with margarine or canola oil.

Ultimately, I agreed to reduce the size of the biscuit in exchange for getting the green light to use unsalted butter in them. Debbie figured out how to make bulk biscuit dough in the stand mixer, and she had those beauties rolled out, cut, and trayed up in no time. The real magic happened at around 6:30 on a dark winter morning. Debbie had baked biscuits for the breakfast trays, and we were going to deliver the first ones to the mother-and-baby unit. These women had faced one of the most physically and emotionally taxing events of their lives and, as a result, were entitled to *two* of these biscuits with jam (it *was* a Smucker's packet, but one step at a time). We all felt like Santa's elves as we quietly delivered breakfast trays, excitedly whispering to those exhausted moms about the freshly baked biscuits that we had for them that morning. The toasty, buttery smell of freshly baked things wafted around the whole unit, bringing warmth and comfort to the sterile hospital environment. Every single weary mom's eyes brightened up when she learned that we had baked something fresh on-site that both looked and smelled *good*. In fact, one mom asked for the tray she had just refused after learning that there was scratch-made freshly baked goods on there for her.

When the tray collection staff returned to the kitchen, they reported a shower of compliments and gratitude from the moms. One of the delivery staff told me that there was not one biscuit left on any of the trays she collected, which is never the case for the limp and defeated toast that is served almost every day. When asked how it felt to serve those biscuits for breakfast, the staff all responded enthusiastically, with big smiles. We cannot dismiss how good it feels to offer something truly wholesome and delicious to somebody in need of nourishment. These were those moments when I saw the chain of human connection come back to life. We knew the man who milled the grain into flour, Debbie had formed and portioned out all of the dough, the staff served those biscuits with pride, and we all received a warm, enthusiastic response. Now, it's clearly more effort to produce this fresh biscuit than it is to produce the toast, but if every single one of those biscuits gets eaten and just under half of that toast gets wasted, which option is better?

Though chefs think dieticians are restrictive joy killers and dieticians think chefs are reckless dispensers of fat and salt, I really wanted to build a bridge between me and the group of dieticians who worked at The Scarborough Hospital. I wanted to understand where the pain points were for them and what they'd like to serve. I really, honestly wanted to help. So I cooked a bunch of food that I'd like to see on patient trays, full of freshness, colour, and some notion of the season, and I invited the dieticians for a taste and a chat. I spent most of the time listening and scribbling down notes as fast as I could. It was very clear to me that they each had a very personal issue with the current state of hospital food and that they don't often get the chance to talk about it. Ultimately, though, the overwhelming consensus was that this group of dieticians were really tired of apologizing to patients. They know the kinds of foods that patients should be eating, and they also know that the hospital doesn't serve those foods. As I walked back to my office after that meeting, I started thinking about how hard it must be to do your job when you can't stand behind what you serve and you're constantly apologizing about what you're offering. The dieticians can't do much more than watch as the responsibility of feeding patients falls on their family members, who have to figure out how to get there three times a day with food. For some, especially those with precarious employment, it isn't possible to miss work, buy or prepare food, and shell out their hourly wage to park their car. This means already marginalized and quite likely malnourished people are staying that way. The final insult? If you're a working person paying your taxes and insurance premiums, you've already paid for that inedible meal.

Eating locally ties us to a place. It gives us roots in the local community and makes us think about how we're connected to other people. One of the primary goals of my Greenbelt funding was to get more local food onto patient plates, but before I could do that, I first needed to get a sense of where the current food was coming from. At the time, the hospital used Sysco, a U.S.-based global distributor of virtually every item that a food service operation needs to function. From mop heads to onions to cheesecake mix to the paper boxes to pack them all up in, Sysco is your one-stop shop for everything related to food service. They're convenient, and their prices are very competitive. It is obvious that Sysco's top priority is supplying as much product to as many food service operations as they can. But Sysco is not looking to build a more sustainable food system; in fact, their business is solidly based on the unsustainability of our current food system.

Purchasers in institutions have never been very particular about where inventory comes from. Their focus is on price and the required specs for meals. Purchasing food is generally treated no differently than purchasing cleaning supplies or linens. The shift towards locally sourced food ingredients created a pretty sizeable challenge for the likes of Sysco and other broadline distributors, and in these early days, our Sysco rep couldn't tell us anything about where a product was produced, whether it was a prepared food or a raw ingredient. Their own inventory management system did not have the capacity to track the origin of any item, though it feels important to mention that this was because nobody was asking for this information.

I don't mean to vilify broadline distributors, but after having observed their process and capacity around making this kind of change, I know for sure that their investment in local food is largely a knee-jerk response to the market, not an expression of any core values. Why is this distinction important? Because it informs the degree to which they are really willing to invest in changing their inventory management and operating procedures. Their approach simply treats local food like a specialty item, which I suppose is a fine place to start, but things quickly revert to the default operating philosophy. For example, after going through a lengthy process to get one distributor to source Ontario apples for us, I walked by the kitchen and saw staff putting away cases of Washington apples. I got on the phone with our supplier to find out what had gone wrong. They told me that they didn't have any Ontario apples in stock and that their system's default was to send whatever they did have in stock, which were apples from Washington. Fair enough, I suppose, but this was in October, which is the height of apple season in Ontario.

The disconnect here seems to be partly due to scale. These broadline suppliers are institutions themselves, and if you want to change one element in an institution's process, you have to be ready to change a number of other things about the operating system to make it work. Many third-party operators and broadline distributors broker their deals with farmers and producers at the national level. In some cases, becoming an approved supplier with one of these companies requires a producer to be able to fulfill orders from British Columbia to the Maritimes. They have to be producing very large volumes of food, which means having farms with hundreds if not thousands of acres of the same crop. We know that this monoculture approach to farming is damaging to the land and often renders it less productive and dependent on chemical inputs after a few seasons. Moreover, this procurement flies directly in the face of the smaller, more sustainable, regional food systems that we are trying to build and support. In the early days, these big purchasers didn't even know how to find small, local farmers; they didn't have those connections nor the knowledge to manage inventory that is harvested to order. In this world, a tomato is a tomato, and the only thing you need to know about it is how much it costs.

So, with no sourcing information coming from Sysco, I decided to take matters into my own hands. I took my winter jacket to work and spent that July day in the freezer with our entire inventory list, scouring packages and looking for any details about where the thing had come from. Virtually none of the boxes of food held any information at all about the source of the ingredients inside. It was very clear to me that this was not information that was of any use to anyone along this food chain. Boxes would say meaningless things like "Proudly warehoused in Hamilton, Ontario," or "Assembled in Canada." On virtually all of the cases of food from national and international brands, delivered to us by a national distributor, there was no mention of provenance. Those cardboard boxes housed a lot of prepared food containing countless ingredients, many of which were highly processed and lab-made, and if I couldn't get information on where the recognizable food ingredients were from, the task of finding the origins of the polysorbate 80, propyl gallate, and potassium bromate seemed completely outrageous. It was there, in that freezer in Scarborough, that I watched the local food movement get smacked in the face by the cemented realities of the global industrial food system.

All told, there were only about 70 of the 470 inventory items with any mention of the point of origin on food ingredients, which is about 15 percent. Of that 70, only about 40 were sourced in Ontario, which is about 9 percent of the total inventory. This meant that 85 percent of the food that was being utilized by the institution contained no information about where it had come from. I realize that this is just one snapshot of one moment in one hospital kitchen, but institutions everywhere rely on broadline suppliers, and the realities of other institutions are not far from this one.

As I started to try to put more local food onto this hospital menu, I realized quickly that one of the biggest challenges would be procurement. Currently, institutional kitchens order everything they need from two to three large suppliers. Orders were mostly placed online and arrived the next day, often shrink-wrapped on a skid. It was convenient, and with a standardized menu, ordering was repetitive, predictable, and relatively easy for one person to manage. It became clear to me that it was unrealistic for most institutions to develop relationships with local farmers individually, and cutting through red tape to get cheques issued to farmers would be a full-time job.

Enter 100km Foods. At the time, Paul Sawtell and Grace Mandarano had just gotten their local food distribution idea off the ground. They wanted to increase access to local food for Toronto restaurants and had built a model that connected chefs in the city to small family farms in Southern Ontario. Restaurants received a weekly list of available in-season food items, food was harvested to order, and chefs paid one supplier. Because their entire inventory was built on sustainability and accessibility, chefs looking for locally grown food now had a reliable, trustworthy source. I knew immediately that 100km Foods was the only way for me to get a model of bureaucracy like a hospital to start purchasing from local suppliers. Due diligence for purchasing in public institutions in Ontario requires three quotes from vendors for a purchase over a certain dollar figure. This allows for some comparative shopping and keeps spending as transparent and accountable as possible. Usually a procurement officer in an institution is given the criteria for the items to be purchased, and they seek out the required three quotes from different vendors. I was always open to using other vendors, provided they had the same values and practices as 100km Foods, but three vendors who could meet our requirements didn't exist. 100km Foods was (and largely remains) the only vendor who could provide the food we were looking for, with the values and relationships we were trying to foster. Administrators would always ask me if 100km Foods was actually the right supplier for us to use or if they were just my friends. The truth is that they're both. In the decade or so that we've spent trying to rebuild the food system, we've become very good friends, sharing all of the success and failure along the way. Remember we're also trying to rebuild human connection here. Our local food system is stronger because we are personally connected to each other.

Buying locally sourced food is not just about purchasing a thing. It's about reinvesting in the chain of hands required to move food from field to kitchen to table. The folks at 100km Foods share my values about the need to rebuild our food system in a way that pays farmers fairly to grow food well and shrinks the gap between producer and consumer. The 100km Foods inventory list tells a story about direct farm connections, with unparalleled transparency. "Our farm partners set their own prices and we mark up from there," Grace told me. "It has been a true partnership from the beginning, marked by mutual respect and understanding." *This* is how I want to spend public money, to both buy product and nurture a more sustainable food system. This model lets us invest in people and relationships by making investments in food.

In my effort to make the money work with local food, I spent a lot of time combing through the price lists of both our large-scale produce distributor and 100km Foods. It was very encouraging to see that many of the prices on the 100km list were negligibly different than the prices we were already paying for imported, conventionally grown, mostly industrial food. 100km offers both conventionally and organically grown food, with clear information on their order sheet about each product. At the time, this was my low-hanging fruit — these were my opportunities to make change in a way that didn't mess with the budgets. One of these items was quick-cook oatmeal. One afternoon, I discovered that the price per unit of quick cook Quaker oats from our distributor was just pennies more than the quick cook oats available from K2 Milling in Tottenham, Ontario. The folks at K2 were relatively new on the scene and had resurrected a dormant milling operation out of a deep commitment to locally grown grains. We instantly made the switch. After our first breakfast delivery, I realized there was a small hitch: staff told us the grind on the oats was a bit too large for patients who had issues with chewing and swallowing. I got on the phone to see if Grace could ask the folks at K2 to run these oats through the mill one more time to break them down a little bit more. Grace responded enthusiastically, telling me that the K2 team would do whatever they could to get their grains onto hospital patient trays. We put this smaller grind of oats on the menu to rave reviews from both patients and support staff. Quaker and Sysco could never have done something like this for us.

Another time, I wanted to swap the bag of apple slices that had been rinsed in a chemical (to prevent them from turning brown) for a whole apple. No bag, no weird chemical bath, just an apple. We got some delicious Honeycrisp apples in from 100km Foods, but they were quite large, and the dietician team was concerned about portion size, particularly for diabetic patients. So once again, I got on the phone with Grace to see if the farmer who provided these apples had smaller ones that we could get — ideally, an apple the size of four to five bites. Grace followed up to say that Torrie Warner, who grew the apples, had small number-three apples that would be perfect. He was particularly delighted to have a buyer for these apples, which were too small for the regular market and going to waste. The number-three apples were the perfect size for us, and some of them still even had leaves attached! We were creating a market for a product that would have otherwise not been sold, and I loved that an institution could support agriculture this way.

I'd never considered the farmer-to-patient relationship and had no idea that farmers would be over the moon with excitement that their food was being served to hospital patients. Every farmer I spoke to about supplying our hospital was delighted to work with us and happy to adjust their production to suit our requirements. I realized very quickly that these farmers were like wallflowers at the school dance: they were just waiting to be asked.

Even with our new suppliers in place, developing and implementing our new menus was slow going. Take, for instance, a simple breakfast. Because of infection control policies, no entree plate can escape the sweaty dome covering as it makes its way through the building to a patient. It is this fateful, humid ride that results in soggy toast and wilted vegetables. And to make matters worse, for whatever reason, the toaster we had was a refurbished coffee shop bagel toaster, which only toasted one side! We couldn't do toast properly, and I wanted to just take it off the menu. What made sense to me was to lean in to what we did have and create menu items that would benefit from a bit of extra steamy heat en route to patients. For a breakfast option, eggs are my first choice, and my thoughts went straight to a frittata. We could pull it out of the oven just a bit before it was finished, and the steam from under that dome would finish the job, ensuring that frittata arrived fluffy and perfectly cooked.

A swap like this might be common sense, but it's still far from simple: the labour for toasting bread sits in a budget line for assembly, but the labour to make a frittata lives in a budget line for production. Ideally, I'd just take the assembly line labour and add it to the production budget . . . but we didn't know how long it would take to prep and cook that frittata and whether it was more than the time allotted to make the toast. And, of course, I wanted to use good, well-raised, whole eggs, but it takes much longer to crack fresh eggs than it does to pour liquid egg from a carton. So I had to do a timed trial run, and I cracked the 210 eggs we needed for breakfast, then set up the frittatas in hotel pans with onions and red peppers for service. From pulling the eggs out of the fridge to wiping down the counter afterwards, the whole effort took me 90 minutes, which was luckily just about the same time it took to make the toast. Debbie cooked the frittatas for breakfast the next morning, and we served it with a carrot muffin, to enthusiastic praise from patients.

As luck would have it, Paul from 100km Foods told me that the Mennonite farm that produces the eggs could provide us with liquid eggs. I was delighted and chuckled at the irony that this level of modern convenience was coming from a population of people focused on adhering to older customs. They were giving me a product created with traditional wisdom in a format that embraces the future. The Mennonite liquid eggs came in a 20 litre bag, as opposed to the individual litre cartons that we got from our other supplier. I appreciated the reduction in waste, purchased one-litre liquid measuring cups, and banished all limp toast from our kitchen.

When strawberry season hit, it seemed a perfect time to jump into local, seasonal eating. Instead of the canned applesauce that had been going on the tray, we were going to serve fresh strawberries. We worked out the cost and portion — four strawberries per person — with the dietician team, and thankfully, this was one of those situations where food that is locally in season is quite affordable. The next question was about the green tops: should they stay or should they go? I thought they made a pretty lovely handle to deliver that sweet fruit to your mouth, but there was some concern that they would be a choking hazard. But if we were going to take the tops off, we needed to find a way to get that bit of labour into the budget. Luckily, Susan Bull, the wonderful director of nutrition services, had bought a couple of strawberry hullers to make the process move more quickly. It's important to remember that nothing exists in isolation in institutions . . . or in life, for that matter. If you want to trim off the tops and put fresh strawberries on the tray, you have to make changes to the purchasing, receiving, preparation, and waste disposal systems. One simple menu change can require a handful of other back-end changes. The messy endurance of this is not for the faint of heart.

As soon as the strawberries arrived, Hung, the friendly and hardworking receiver at The Scarborough Hospital, came by with a cart holding six flats right from

Barrie Hill Farms in Simcoe County, just a couple hours north of us. He could see the excitement in my face, and it was so nice to see his own face light up when he tasted the berry I offered him. I asked Hung to please put the strawberries in the produce fridge for the prep team the following morning, and he looked at me blankly. I paused and looked around at the three walk-in fridges and two walk-in freezers lining the walls around us. Then it hit me. I smiled at him and said, "There *is* no produce fridge, is there, Hung?" He smiled at me and shook his head. Three walk-in fridges and none of that space was used to store produce. I found a Sharpie, wrote PRODUCE on a piece of masking tape, and stuck it to the door of a virtually empty fridge. "There," I said, "*now* we have a produce fridge." There were many days when I would drive home discouraged and not sure if our efforts were worthwhile. And then there were other days when re-establishing a fridge to store fresh produce felt nothing short of revolutionary.

My heart raced with excitement as I phoned Morris Gervais, the farmer who grew those lovely strawberries, to tell him that his strawberries were going out on patient trays. Morris is a second-generation farmer who also grows blueberries, raspberries, and asparagus on his family's farm in Springwater, Ontario. He chuckled on the phone and said, "So, you mean to tell me that you're actually using Ontario money to buy Ontario food to feed Ontario patients?!" I laughed and exclaimed, "YES! That's exactly what we're doing, and I'm going to put that on a T-shirt someday." What a perfectly tidy concept: let's use local money to buy local food to support local people. We had a long way to go, but the four trimmed strawberries that went out on each patient tray that day was a fantastic start.

In addition to being seasonal, locally sourced, and scratch-made, it was important that our menus be culturally diverse and accommodate dietary restrictions. These last two bits really made for a next-level challenge. I'd already learned at The Stop that sometimes I needed to soften some of my rigidity around prioritizing local, sustainably sourced food to accommodate other values like cultural diversity, dietary restrictions, and veganism and vegetarianism. When I was working on these projects, dietary accommodations were still relatively new, and since then, I've seen considerable progress, but there's still a ways to go. I still rarely see the thoughtfulness that is required to first understand who the population is that you're feeding and to then build menus that are inclusive and accessible to everyone in that group. I see so many vegetarian meals that just have a chunk of tofu substituted for whatever animal product may have been there, and vegan meals that are dry because the sauce that had dairy in it has just been left off. I also see a lot of half-hearted attempts at cooking foods from a particular cultural group. I really want kitchens to do the research, find two to three recipes, and compare them to each other to find similarities in ingredients and method. Find out if there's a member of the team from that cultural tradition and ask for their input. If you're serving food from a culture that is not yours, it's important to do the best job you can to ensure both enjoyment and respect. Serving food that is culturally familiar and appropriate for a person's needs is a great way to ensure that it gets eaten, and it sends a message of care and belonging to the patients.

Accommodating these needs is most affordably and effectively done in an institution that has invested in scratch cooking and the skill of its team, who can make adjustments as required. There are some exceptions, though. Kosher meals need to be prepared in a kosher kitchen, so they are usually ordered in from a kosher catering company. These meals come wrapped very intentionally and are served that way to guests, who will unwrap the meals themselves to keep the kosher chain unbroken. Halal meals, however, can be prepared on-site, as long as staff observe some specific guidelines around the sourcing of the meat, avoid certain restricted ingredients (cheese made with animal rennet, vanilla extract with alcohol), and maintain separate utensils for service. With a large Muslim population in Scarborough, we really needed to produce good halal meals. Before I arrived at the hospital, they had already asked a local imam to come into the kitchen to make sure that they were handling food correctly, and he offered advice on some cooking processes and colour-coding utensils to keep them separate. He was quite confident about our ability to serve the Muslim community well from our kitchen. I was encouraged to hear this, as this is precisely the kind of community engagement that we need in public institutions. We were able to get our hands on some halal meat and put one halal entrée on the menu each day. With one vegetarian option available as well, we were able to offer a balanced halal patient menu.

But even for those not bound by religious edicts, culturally appropriate meals are essential, as some cursory rounds with patients showed me. One day, I chatted with an older Pakistani man who had just suffered a stroke. His adult daughter was there, holding out the tuna sandwich that was served for lunch so that he could take bites of it. They were both quite friendly and open to chatting with us, and I asked if he had ever eaten a tuna sandwich before. He shook his head no, and in his slurred, post-stroke speech, he also told me that in his culture, applesauce wasn't a food. We chatted with another patient who was saving the little slips of paper with the details about the meal that come on each tray. He told us that he would use them as guidelines for what to eat when he got back home. Now, in theory, this is quite exciting: those tray talkers have the potential to be an effective teaching tool. On the ground, however, it was a disaster. This patient was an older man with Southeast Asian heritage, and this process would have him hunting down cans of tuna and loaves of refined white bread, *because that's what the hospital was feeding him*. But the truth is whatever traditional food that was likely being cooked in his house was much better for him to eat than a white bread tuna sandwich. And finally, we spoke with a South Asian man in his 40s who had just had a heart attack. I noticed that he hadn't touched his lunch tray, and I asked him how he would feel about getting a plate of dal and rice. His eyes lit up, and he sat up in bed to ask me if he could actually get a plate of dal and rice. I apologized for even bringing it up, knowing full well that I couldn't make good on that promise. But that was a great lesson in gauging the patient population's appetite for culturally diverse foods. Ultimately, we managed to develop recipes for dal and rice, jerk chicken, congee, a Moroccan vegetable dish, and a sesame noodle salad for the patient menu. As an added bonus, patients from other cultural groups enjoyed the different flavour offerings of these dishes as a welcome reprieve from the standard meat-starch-veg fare — culturally appropriate food is not exclusively for people from that cultural group! This diversity makes for a delicious and varied dining experience for anyone who receives a meal tray, and it enables hospital menus to reflect the community they serve.

As more of the local harvest arrived in the kitchen, I had a hunch that when cooks actually cooked again, we would blow everyone's minds. All of our new recipes were developed and costed to stay within the current budget. Although challenging, this was easier for food ingredients than for labour. I was really curious about whether it was even possible for the physical kitchen space to pull off a scratch-made meal in its current state. I wasn't sure whether this was just a matter of training and some new equipment or if there was something else standing in the way. I wanted to test our capacity by bringing in a guest chef to cook lunch with Debbie and me, to see what might be possible with a more skilled team at the counter.

It was a cold February morning when Chef Rodney Bowers joined us in the kitchen. We were going to cook a completely scratch-made, locally sourced lunch for all of the patients on the regular menu that day. Rod is a beloved Toronto chef who has brought the city cherished restaurants like The Rosebud Café and Hey Meatball, plus he's something of a media darling, with a thriving television career. He's also a dear friend and ally and one helluva charmer. I invited Rod because I knew he'd get it and that he'd be up for this little experiment with me.

I had gotten some local turkeys, and we ordered all sorts of root vegetables from 100km Foods. We had local mushrooms and apples and some beautiful frozen sour cherries. Rod immediately got to work with Debbie, slicing mushrooms for a consommé, while I dressed the turkeys for the oven. I peeled and diced beets and potatoes to roast for a warm root veg salad, and Rod made a quick pickle of some beets and carrots. Debbie put together an apple and sour cherry crumble, and we all laughed and worked joyfully. I really loved seeing this kitchen in full operation; it was like another version of itself! All of the counters were being used, there were bright and colourful things on trays, and the team was fired up to cook some real food!

Staff with offices nearby followed their noses to the kitchen, with a bit of wonder and curiosity on their faces, asking *what* we were doing in there. I smiled, put my hand on one woman's shoulder, and said, "Believe it or not, we're COOKING!" Rather than the usual institutional mealtime fragrance — a sickly combination of vegetable soup and disinfectant — they were smelling roasting vegetables and caramelization and the sweet cinnamon in our fruit crumble. Good food was already drawing people together.

As we got down to the wire, we raced around getting food set on the conveyor belt line where patient trays were assembled for meal service. We put a little note from Rod on the trays, mentioning that everything was scratch-made and locally sourced. The plates were bright and alive, with food that looked delicious and drew you in. There was real, honest flavour and the distinct taste of care and attention. I loved seeing Rod on the line with the tray assembly team and savoured how obviously proud and happy everyone was about the meal we were serving that day. Rod and I excitedly went up to the orthopaedic ward and delivered a tray to a patient with a broken leg. We explained what we were doing and that he was the first one to receive this awesome local lunch. This patient couldn't believe his luck and exclaimed about how delicious the tray looked. The patient in the bed beside him asked urgently whether he would be receiving this tray too, and it was really nice to finally be proud to say yes.

Our team reported notably clean plates when the trays came back down, and there was even a bit of food left over for the staff to taste. I wanted the team to see what was possible in that kitchen and for them to know that I wanted to help them get there. Many of our staff came up to me later with all sorts of thoughtful ideas for how to adjust our operations to make meals like this happen. That service was definitely a hustle, and we were all pretty exhausted, but in the deep of an Ontario winter, we served an all-local lunch made from scratch for hospital patients. And when I reconciled numbers at the end of service, I learned that we spent only an additional $0.33 per person for ingredients for that day's lunch. It's a relatively small investment for an exponentially better dining experience. But yes, it's an investment, and we do have to spend some more money on patient meals.

I recently ran into Rod and told him about having just written about our time together cooking lunch at The Scarborough Hospital. His face lit up, and he reminded me that the woman who works on the internal hospital switchboard told us that in 21 years, our lunch was the first patient meal that received no complaints. "That's a pretty clear message, if you ask me," Rod exclaimed. I haven't worked in any institution long enough to get hard, reliable data about the impacts of the new food culture, so feedback like this is gold. I've learned that hospital administrators are more compelled by the idea of improving the patient experience with better food than they are convinced of the need to invest in more sustainable, wholesome food systems. Frankly, I'm happy to jump on whichever angle gets my foot in the door.

This experiment made it clear that with the right resources, skilled, motivated staff could produce amazing food. Unfortunately, the industrial food regime hasn't only been undermining the food served, it has been undermining the human labour who provide it. Most hospital labour is unionized, and unions ensure better working conditions and secure, livable wages for workers. With a reduction in wages not on the table, when administrators see expenses that need to be trimmed, cost cutters reduce the need for any human labour at all, finding a food supply that is cooked, portioned, and requires only a thaw or reheat to make it ready to serve.

Though there may have been labour savings, these changes still come at a cost. Retherm units cost $40,000 to $60,000 each, and the average hospital has at least a dozen of them. The lifespan of one of these units is five years. Some can last up to 10 years, but with compromised functioning after five. And all that frozen food has to be stored, which means a massive amount of refrigerator and freezer space is required. I find it really hard to believe that this energy guzzling system is still cheaper than paying human beings to cook food. A civil servant friend of mine suggested that this might make sense on a spreadsheet, because the full cost of the hydro to maintain those cool temperatures often does not live on the food services budget line. Once again, we've found ourselves in a discussion about not paying the full costs of allegedly "more affordable" food.

In my transition to scratch-made cooking, I realized that there was a substantial gap between the cooking skills that currently existed on the kitchen team and the cooking skills required to serve the menu that I had in mind. When "efficiency" came in, most of the actual culinary work went out. "Cooking" now meant plating frozen, portioned food onto trays for patients or opening vacuum-sealed bags of soups and sauces to warm up for meal service. In some cases, staff would thaw frozen, cooked meat and add something powdered to make a sauce. They would thaw cut frozen vegetables and serve everything over a bed of steamed white rice, boiled pasta, or mashed potatoes that started from something dry. There's lots of reheating and rehydrating going on but not a whole lot of what I understood as cooking. I spent a lot of time considering this. What was the definition of cooking? Does it explicitly start with raw ingredients? Does it matter if ingredients come out of a package? If we say simply that cooking is about preparing food to eat, then I suppose what's happening in institutional kitchens still qualifies. But *is* that cooking? I have always felt that cooking involved a generous intention and worked with some cultivated skill using good raw ingredients to produce a plate of food. You don't imagine that you need to articulate that cooking is about producing food that will actually benefit people's bodies. I knew without a doubt that every member of that kitchen team had the best and most generous intentions about serving patients. But I also know that from a skills and ingredients perspective, they had been set up for failure by the powers that be.

In hindsight, it was wildly ambitious to imagine that we would completely rebuild the menu, the kitchen, and the skills of the team within the yearlong time frame of this project. While most of the teaching and coaching happened along the way, we simply ran out of time to reskill and upskill the kitchen labour team. I did manage to sneak in a few knife-skills workshops with the prep team, but much more methodical effort was required for an effective reskilling. We needed more time to be able to augment the skills of the team and then implement new labour processes, but all I could do at the time was lay the groundwork for this kind of skills building in the future.

I didn't just want better food, I also wanted better work. Considering those returned patient trays headed straight for the trash and to all those people not getting properly fed, there's also an emotional cost to consider. At the time, the staff members had been working in that hospital kitchen for an average of between 15 and 20 years. What is it like working for that many years knowing that you're not being effective? I understand that the job is secure and the pay is fair, but shouldn't our work also make us feel good? On a day-to-day level, their role had been industrialized, stripped of creativity, agency, and opportunities for growth. But they also had families and mortgages to consider, and many of them felt quite lucky to have the secure full-time jobs they did.

Over the 12 months that I was at The Scarborough Hospital, we did notice an increase in staff morale. It's purely anecdotal, but Susan, who had known many of these folks for almost 25 years, noticed that there were more smiles and body language that was more open and happier. It was clear that the staff felt prouder to serve patients better food. They worked harder to get more done during their shifts; they felt better about the work they were doing; many even started making changes to the way their families ate too. People don't just need their jobs for a steady income: they need meaning and purpose as well. Cheap, industrial food not only extinguishes the spirit of the people it's served to, it extinguishes the spirit of the people serving that food.

As part of the reskilling project, I decided to take our whole kitchen team to a fine-dining restaurant to see how that kitchen ran. I wanted them to see a team of cooks working with whole ingredients and a kitchen that constantly had a stockpot going. Plus, I thought it would be nice for these folks to be spoiled and treated to some fancy, delicious food in a beautiful setting. I reached out to my pal John Horne, who was then the chef at Canoe, a wonderfully posh restaurant on the 54th floor of a Toronto bank tower. I'd hoped for a little tour of the kitchen, a chat with John, and then maybe a little snack, but it turned into much more than that. John had brought in Canadian proteins to show our team the kinds of ingredients the restaurant works with. He had a whole halibut and some wild geese on the counter, much to everyone's delight. All three of their large stock kettles were bubbling away, and every single member of that team welcomed us warmly. We sat in the dining room with a killer view of the harbourfront and were served sliders and lobster rolls while John told the team how important our project was. We rolled ourselves out of that dining room, everyone stuffed full and feeling nicely puffed up from our experience.

Debbie was particularly taken with what she saw and asked lots of questions. As the lead cook at the hospital, she was fascinated by the workings of this restaurant kitchen and how everyone did their jobs. John very generously invited her to come and cook with them one day. She eagerly took him up on their offer, and a couple of weeks later, I received a photo of Debbie rolling pasta in the Canoe kitchen, with the giddiest look on her face. She returned to the hospital full of inspiration and excitement, and it was a beautiful thing to see. John and his team had really welcomed her in as a cook. The contexts are different, but on some level, cooks are cooks, and part of what I was trying to do was pull back the curtain between restaurants and institutions. Debbie was a very skilled cook, but a lot of her talent lay dormant in the service of the highly reheated menu she had to serve. What she really needed was the chance to recognize herself in those restaurant cooks and develop those skills. One morning shortly after her magical day at Canoe, I walked into the kitchen to find Debbie in her usual spot but wearing a chef's jacket instead of her usual scrubs. I smiled at her and said, "Good morning, Chef!" I asked her if she bought that jacket for herself, and she said no, there were always some in the changeroom, but now she felt like she deserved to wear it.

A couple of months into our project at The Scarborough Hospital, Jessica Leeder from the *Globe and Mail* visited to learn more about what we were doing. She had lots of questions and was really interested in our mission. We got a full-page spread — some pretty prime real estate — in the Saturday *Globe*. (Sadly, it was likely the only time in my life I'll be in a centrefold, and I was wearing a hairnet.) Full of excitement, I floated into the kitchen on Monday morning. But the tone I encountered was much more solemn and quiet than I had hoped it would be. Susan told me that the team was stung by all of the disparaging comments made about the food that was being served before I had arrived, and they felt like I had manipulated things to position myself as a saviour, swooping in to fix a problem. I immediately went to speak to Debbie and the team, and everyone was quite frosty with me. I tried to explain what I think happened and to reinforce how much I valued and respected that whole team. But these folks were hurt and felt betrayed, and that shut down communication with me.

I was disappointed that we weren't all celebrating this fantastic feature in a national newspaper, but I needed to understand the team's perspective and my contribution to these hurt feelings. In a newspaper feature about a project to improve hospital food, the obvious villain is the food itself. And it's much sexier to talk about a chef who comes in to fix the problem than it is to talk about the dedicated kitchen team who has been doing the very best they can with what is available. But the team took all of the negative comments about the food personally and didn't feel as though their perspective or their contributions were acknowledged. They were working really hard, with noble intentions, and did not need to have their work criticized in a national newspaper. I honestly didn't see this coming. This was definitely my problem to fix, but it was also a real surprise.

I realized that the food and nutrition team didn't have a clear sense of how important this project was or how quickly the good food movement was gaining traction. My colleagues in the hospital kitchen weren't part of our food community yet. I realized that my task was to try to build that connection and help this awesome team know just how much they're valued and supported by me and by a larger group of good food advocates. Back at my desk, I opened my email to compose a new message. I added every ally and contributor to our good food movement that I knew, including cooks, bakers, brewers, winemakers, professors, activists, community workers, politicians, doctors, journalists, artisans, farmers, and restauranteurs. I titled the message "Our Hospital Project Needs a Cheering Section" and asked each of them to take a moment to send the team a message to welcome them to this community of people who encouraged and supported each other in the good-food fight. The messages poured in, and they were wonderful. One of my favourites was from my dear friends Lulu Cohen Farnell and David Farnell, who make thousands of school lunches a day from their Real Food for Real Kids kitchen: "You have our unflinching support and immense gratitude and respect for taking up this challenge. We're rooting for you every step of the way!"

I received more than 50 of these amazing messages and posted them on a brightly coloured notice board for the team to read. I wasn't sure whether they were impressed at all, but a few days later, one of the staff came to my office and commented on how nice one of the messages was. And then someone else did too. I started to see more staff standing in front of the board, reading those notes, and I could feel the frost start to melt. Thankfully, the team began to trust me again. I thought a lot about how this could have been avoided, and what I could have done differently. This was an important lesson to slow down and remember that not everyone is always on the same page as I am. I'm an ambitious list-maker who wants to get stuff done, but I have to make space for the things I don't know about and for others to have their own responses. When you're trying to steer a large operation in a new direction, this is really important, and I was very careful to avoid this mistake in the future.

One March a few years ago, I was planting tomato seeds to sprout indoors. A farmer friend visited me and casually commented that "food is the way we receive nutrients from the earth." I stopped, my eyes widening. I'd never even considered that there were nutrients in the earth that I needed to live and that food is the delivery mechanism. This is perhaps our most profound connection with the natural world, and it's one some of us have lost altogether. Food is much more than fuel, and eating is much more than filling the tank . . . our food is our life force, it's what tethers us to the earth.

So I decided to go a step further in showing the team they were a vital part of the chain of hands that moves food from field to tray. The task of reworking the procurement, receiving, preparation, service, and waste management of hospital food services is giant, with more moving parts than anyone really knows about. I was asking them to do their jobs completely differently, and I could offer little more than my promise that we were doing the right thing. I knew that the good place to start would be to get the staff themselves to understand why we were doing something like this. I wanted to hopefully ignite a spark inside of them and inspire them with the good food vision for the future.

Susan and I decided to use some of our Greenbelt

development dollars to take the whole team on a field trip. There was no question that the right place for us to visit was The New Farm in Creemore, Ontario, because if we were going to revalue all of the hands involved in moving food from field to kitchen to tray, then that starts at the farm. Gillian Flies and Brent Preston are both deeply committed to rebuilding our food system and have decided that for them, it starts with the soil. Brent and Gill are valued comrades in the struggle for a better food system and had just turned over their fifth season on their organic farm; what they and their team have been able to accomplish in that time is nothing short of astounding. If the apocalypse hits, I'll start making my way directly towards The New Farm.

They welcomed our team with their signature warmth and hospitality. At the time, they were raising chickens, and Gill had pulled three birds from the freezer for us to have for lunch. These beauties were thawed and waiting for me in their kitchen, and Brent already had the Green Egg going to grill them up. Gill pressed some garlic and two handfuls of mixed herbs from the farm into my hands and asked me to prep the chickens for lunch while she and Brent had a little welcome chat with the team outside. I worked away happily, doing very little to those well-raised birds. I cut out the spines and spatchcocked them, which flattens the bird out into one layer for more even cooking on the grill. Plus, more surface area meant more parts of that chicken could get coated with delicious flavour and grill marks.

Through the screen door, I could hear Brent speaking to the group about our friendship, our shared values, and the tight community that has emerged as a result of our commitment to living these values. Then he welcomed that team of cooks, tray assembly and delivery staff, dishwashers, receivers, and dieticians into our community, expressing gratitude and delight that the numbers were increasing so rapidly. In just a few minutes, Brent did something that I had been struggling for months to do. He connected this fledgling hospital food project to a deeper movement of people actively involved in rebuilding our food system. He let this group of institutional food service staff know that they were a part of something much bigger than just us, and that he was hopeful for what the future might hold. As I rubbed a garlic herb paste on those chickens, happy tears began to stream down my face, and I was thankful for Brent and his generous kindness. That moment — standing in the kitchen, elbow deep in chickens, looking out at the field, listening to Brent and Gill warmly welcome my team while having a very happy, albeit messy cry — is one that will stay with me forever. And I was struck by yet another example of the desire for a farmer-to-patient relationship and how seriously grateful farmers are to know that their food is being served to hospital patients.

The New Farm is famous for a number of things, their salad greens among them. Like everything on the farm, these greens are planted, tended, harvested, and packaged with care and attention. When you stand there, watching the farm team on their knees working away on those glorious rows of tender lettuces, you understand the magnitude of the labour involved, *and* you really want to eat those salad greens! They had set up a row of picnic tables for us and a beautiful table held our grilled chickens, a big salad of New Farm greens with Gill's now-famous vinaigrette, and some cheese and bread from a nearby bakery and dairy. This food was fresh, simple, and full of good, honest flavour. I walked around to see how everyone was enjoying the food. Everyone kept asking me what I did to the chickens, and they had a hard time believing that it was only garlic and herbs from the farm and some canola oil and sea salt. They were convinced that I had sprinkled some magic fairy dust on those birds, and I explained that they were tasting a naturally raised chicken, with more flavour and juiciness than anything a factory farm could ever produce. When they ate the greens, they tasted the pepperiness of arugula and the tender bitterness of baby kale. I can talk and talk about the benefit of local eating and organic growing, but one farm lunch, with its big flavour and deep satisfaction, can do so much more to illustrate the truth of this. It was so joyful to watch my hospital kitchen team holding cones of Mapleton's organic ice cream and walking around the farm with looks of almost childlike curiosity on their faces. In this one visit, almost all of them understood the value and benefit of farm-fresh food.

When we were standing out in the fields by the salad greens, listening to Gill talk about the soil and their investments in enriching its nutrition and biodiversity, one of the tray assembly staff came over to me and asked if we were really going to serve these greens to hospital patients. I smiled at her and told that yes, that was the plan. Her face lit up and she said, "Oh, I will be so proud to serve these greens to our patients!" I choked back more tears, hugged her, and realized that it was happening. This was *working*. As the tour continued, the staff asked questions, tasted warm tomatoes, and really understood what we were trying to do together at the hospital. I honestly felt as though I saw little good food lightbulbs go off above everyone's head at some point. It was nothing short of magical.

That year, The New Farm was growing potatoes, but the potato bugs were particularly fierce. They didn't have enough money to buy netting for all of their plants, and so they lost a whole row of crops. I walked up beside Susan Bull, who was staring out at the rows of potatoes. "My budget just sits in the bank waiting to be spent," she said. "Why can't I just give them that money up front and then have them bring us potatoes all season?" I smiled, put my hand on her shoulder, and said, "There's no reason at all, my dear. And that is an institutional CSA." I thought about community supported agriculture, or, in this case, institutionally supported agriculture, on the drive back home, and although I didn't manage to get this set up in the time I had at the hospital, it's a very viable idea. There's really no reason why we couldn't start pairing up farms with hospitals like this, and it would open up the opportunity for an institution to augment the impact of their purchase without spending any extra money. Public institutions spend millions of dollars a year on food — doesn't it make sense that the majority of that money stay close to home?

In the years since then, The New Farm has created a program called Farms for Change. They throw a big annual concert fundraiser at their farm, and the proceeds from the event go right towards their production of organic food. Throughout the year, The Stop and a few other community food centres receive these vegetables to use in community programming. Communities get good, local, organic produce; The New Farm has financial security for their harvest; and the people who donate enjoy a great event and leave with a tax receipt and a sense that they're tangibly supporting real change: everyone's a winner. Ultimately, we weren't able to make the numbers work to actually start ordering these greens at the hospital, but the response from the team that day got Gill thinking, and she and her team received some grant funding to develop a version of their salad greens that are less intensive to grow and can be sold at a more accessible price, specifically to public institutions. Unfortunately, before it really got off the ground, the grant funding dried up — and with it the space for innovation.

I had arranged for everyone to take home a dozen eggs and a bag of salad greens from the farm, and the team members clamoured to get their goodies, knowing how special and delicious this stuff was. For the next week, I had team members coming up to thank me for the field trip. Many of them had never been to a farm in Canada, and that visit took them back to their childhoods in their home countries. They told me stories about how much their kids enjoyed those eggs and greens and how they wanted to set up a staff purchasing plan from 100km Foods so that they could get some of that good local food into their home kitchens. This was the first time I had ever had a real conversation with some of the staff, and I love even the slightest suggestion that good food helped to create a connection. Everyone who went on the farm trip was a bit changed afterwards. Our project had meaning, and the team felt like they were a part of something special. For me, it wasn't just about the good food or connection to the land; it was about linking staff to the farmers themselves. I hoped that if we started ordering and those bins of greens arrived in the kitchen, the team would remember the hands and faces of the people who grew that food.

In the spring of 2013, after tackling food for patients at The Scarborough Hospital, I got a chance to take on food for everyone else — parents, staff, and visitors — at the Hospital for Sick Children, also known as SickKids, in Toronto. I wasn't initially interested in the job — I wanted to focus on patient food. Then I realized that if a kid is at SickKids, a global leader in paediatric care and research, there's likely something *really* wrong;

otherwise they'd be in the paediatric ward of their neigh-bourhood hospital. And for every not-okay little one in a bed, there are usually two worried grown-ups on-site. I realized that worrying parents and guardians should be eating more than a steady diet of Tim Hortons bagels, and I became excited about making beautiful, nourish-ing food for families. I also remembered the words of my friend and Stop colleague Linor David, who ran the perinatal program: "The best way to take care of a child is to take care of their mama." Obviously this applies to all parents, and I was happy for the reminder that none of us exist in isolation.

The nutrition team at SickKids was incredibly wel-coming, and I spent a lot of time listening and learning about their processes, the challenges, and where they thought opportunities for change were. Tracy Maccarone was the director of the department at the time, and much like Susan Bull at The Scarborough Hospital, she was really open and enthusiastic about what we might be able to accomplish. She also wanted to learn about how she could put more local food into her family's diet. We had many conversations about price and access and debated various ways to make the change work. Tracy wel-comed me into their kitchen, introducing me to Shawn Studholme, their executive chef. Shawn had been at SickKids for a number of years, and he and his team had also endured the waves of budget cuts that the previous decades had brought. Shawn was in charge of retail food production, which was essentially the hospital cafeteria, the Terrace Café. A few other franchises existed on-site to round out the retail food offerings.

There was a small group of six to eight retail cooks producing food daily for the hospital community. Between the hospital itself and the research tower, there were about 3,000 people working in that cluster of buildings, all of whom needed something to eat at some point. There was also a catering operation on-site, and the cooks took care of prep for those orders as well, which were mostly fruit, sweets, and sandwich platters. Our task was to put more local food onto that retail menu and create more fresh, seasonal options for the hospital community.

What I had learned from my time in Scarborough was to be gentle and ease my way into making change with the kitchen team. I knew now to expect some hesitation and skepticism from the team. I focused on making connections and building trust before talking about implementing change. That said, I did have a couple of wonderful early enthusiasts! Rosalina, a powerhouse cold prep cook on the retail team, was responsible for making salads and prepping vegetables for the salad bar. She was also really interested in new flavours and ingredients, so the first thing I did was get a selection of cold-pressed oils and wine vinegars from Pristine Gourmet, a family farm in Norfolk County for her to experiment with. Every morning I'd walk into the kitchen and she would have something new for me to taste. We started getting local produce in, and she turned that salad bar into a gorgeous celebration of the local harvest. It was wonderful to see her eagerness and her pride at how well it was received by our customers. We got some new signage and placed little green tomato icons on all of the salad bar items that were made with local ingredients. Gradually, with some help from our communications team, Rosalina's salad station became quite popular, and we'd consistently see the items labelled with the green tomato sell out. When there's a run on *salad*, you know you're doing something right.

We went through a similar process with the hot prep team, who already made thoughtful, delicious specials every day. I worked with the team to put a bit more scratch cooking and local ingredients into those meals. It seems simple enough to say it, but this included recipe development, testing, costing, reworking ordering, inventory, and receiving procedures, and a deep dive into labour and scheduling. The hot prep team already had a pretty substantial workload, and there wasn't very much room for more, so instead of adding new items to the menu, I focused on reworking the existing menu items. Thankfully, even with this bit of change, more of those little green tomatoes crept over to the hot table.

And while I wasn't there to focus on the patient menu, there's no way I wouldn't poke my head into the patient kitchen. And truthfully it was pretty great. They had a room service–style menu for patients, and while it included things like chicken fingers and fries, it also had pastas, fresh vegetables, and nice-looking fruit. With kids who are sick, the challenge is getting them to eat anything at all, and if that means chicken fingers, so be it. I am reminded of Janice Sorenson's wisdom: "Food is only healthy when eaten." A patient's comfort in the healing process is vital, and it's even more important when it comes to kids. From the emotional experience to the very real heightened vulnerability of those dramatically weaker immune systems, there are extra considerations to take into account. The idea of fresh, organic produce is wonderful, but from an infection control perspective, the possibility of all sorts of creatures nestled into those leaves and entering the hospital is a disaster waiting to happen. I did reach out to Grace at 100km Foods about this, and she was able to steer us towards the farms who were extra diligent in washing their produce after harvesting it.

My work at the SickKids café meant we'd also be feeding hospital staff. In my experience, this is a collection of some of the kindest, most skilled medical professionals anywhere. They're deeply committed to excellent patient care and understand the softness required for good paediatric care. I realized that we could help support patient care by feeding the care team really well. Let's make sure the paediatric cardiologist eats a really good meal before she heads in to operate on an infant's heart. The food served in a hospital needs to support the staff, who in turn provide high-quality care to patients. This is true of every one of our public institutions. While I maintain that properly feeding patients, students, and prisoners should be the top priority, it's curious that we don't ever think about what teachers, doctors, guards, and admin staff are eating.

On the follow-up visit after my sinus surgery, my surgeon and I started talking about the kind of work that I do and about me writing this book, and he said something really interesting. He told me that he had been at that hospital for about 13 years, and one of the things he really misses about food service in the past was the opportunity for conviviality in the cafeteria and dining hall. My doctor told me about his memory of connecting with colleagues over a meal and having the time and space to sit down and eat something delicious before or after performing a surgery. He told me that at one point there was a doctor's dining hall that served good meals. "Now," he said, "my meals are just . . ." I looked up at him and filled in the space, "Some shitty food in a Styrofoam box at your desk?" He smiled and nodded.

People may argue that doctors are paid enough to be able to afford good food for themselves, but I think this doesn't address the real issue, which is about culture and availability. If you're racing between appointments or have only a small window between two surgeries, you need good options available on-site. We need to rebuild more than just the food, we need to rebuild the *culture* of food. A dining hall isn't just a room where people sit at tables to silently scarf down their lunch. A dining hall is a place intentionally built for people to come together and share food. Yes, there's eating, but there's also social connection, a break from the intensity of the work, and a moment to refuel and recharge.

One afternoon at The Scarborough Hospital cafeteria, just past the lineup of cashiers, I held a cooking demo. I had a little burner and was preparing a seasonal vegetable sauté with some goat cheese and fresh herbs. I offered samples to whoever was interested, hoping to pique the interest of some of the nurses and doctors passing by. During the demo, I noticed lots of folks in scrubs and surgical caps racing off with takeout containers of burgers and fries and a can of pop in their hands. My first reaction was disappointment, but then I scolded myself for having such a narrow view. Maybe they had just operated on someone's heart or spent hours reconstructing someone's knee cap. That work is really intense, and maybe a cheeseburger is exactly what they want after an effort like that. I know that oftentimes after an intense service or a long day of tedious prep, tucking into something satisfying like a burger and fries is exactly the right thing. I'm not advocating for the removal of burgers and fries from the menu, but I do think that we should invest in making the best burger and fries we can. Let's make sure that burger patty is made with well-raised beef and without the spongy fillers that we see in so many industrial burger patties. Let's get some real cheese and house-made pickles, and let's cut those fries ourselves, using locally grown potatoes. Let's give them a comfortable place to sit and a real reprieve. Let's care for the people who care for us.

SickKids also received some Greenbelt funding, but with a broader mandate around community engagement than the project in Scarborough. One of my objectives with these grant funds was local food and sustainability programming for the SickKids community, so we decided to hold a local food expo in the atrium of the building. We had created some tent cards with information about the ease and benefits of eating locally on tables in the dining area. We also had a mini version of our weekly farmers' market, with a couple of vendors sampling and selling their honey, mushrooms, bread, and cheese, and a lunch-and-learn session featuring Brent from The New Farm talking about their operation and the benefits of organic growing and eating. Brent and I giggled before the talk, gleefully celebrating what we were sure was the first time a farmer gave a talk about food in a hospital. I loved that the impressively tall light-filled atrium at SickKids was the venue for this kind of important food education: it felt right that staff would have the opportunity to learn about the importance of using organic food in a hospital.

The weekend before the local food expo, I went to the farmers' market to purchase some food supplies for the day. I visited the Vicki's Veggies booth to see Vicki Emlaw, an eighth-generation family farmer in Prince Edward County and generous teacher who joyfully engages with all of the people who visit her farm. Winter had just begun, and I was happy to have her lovingly grown root vegetables for our event. When it was time to settle up the bill, Vicki pulled out her receipt pad and asked who she should make it out to. I smiled at her and said, "SickKids Hospital!" This was the first time she had ever invoiced a hospital for some of her food — I don't usually get charged up about accounting, but this little administrative thing was more real evidence of change.

As Vicki was packing my food into crates, she pressed a bag of the tiniest carrots into my hand. "Take these," she said. "They're crazy sweet!" She had pulled these tiny multicoloured beauties out of the ground before the frost got too serious, so they were small and packed with sweetness. Later that day, I was registering people for the expo, and I offered everyone a carrot. They looked down at the bag of yellow, purple, and orange things in disbelief. "I've never seen carrots that colour!" they said. I encouraged people to reach into the bag, pull out a carrot, and eat it. I was floored to discover just how much coaching was required for people to do something like this. Were they washed? Shouldn't they be peeled? Weren't there any tongs? Then they'd pause with that little carrot in their hand, like it was a cricket or something. Once they mustered up the courage to put the thing in their mouth, they were rewarded with that intense sweetness and their eyes lit up. But I was shocked by the mistrust that was displayed; so much of our basic knowledge about food has been lost over the course of generations that produce in its natural state looks unfamiliar. I was offering carrots

— one of the most popular vegetables ever! — yet somehow people are less suspicious of a bag of "baby" carrots, that are machine cut from larger carrots, rinsed in a chlorine solution, bagged in plastic, and shipped to stores.

At the time, holding a lunch-and-learn session with a farmer in a hospital atrium was a very new thing, and I wasn't sure what the attendance would be, but we had a delicious local lunch prepared and knew that an offer of free food can fill a room. To our delight, the place was packed, and people even stood in the back enjoying a sandwich while Brent spoke. They asked good questions and gave us really positive feedback on the way out. It was a gift to see the excitement and inspiration on the faces of the hospital staff who attended the session, both from eating something fresh and delicious and from listening to the good news story that Brent shared about their farm. It was clear that everyone who left that session had a deeper understanding of what it means to grow food and what we were trying to do with our local food project. Although they went beyond healing the sick, events that promoted new ideas about health on an individual and social level really helped to build a culture of food in the hospital.

Of course, the cafeteria isn't the only game in town when it comes to grabbing something to eat. I remember watching the lineup in front of a Tim Hortons in a hospital I visited once. The line was almost always at least four people deep and contained family members, patients, admin folks, doctors, nurses, someone from maintenance, a construction worker, and volunteers, all waiting in line for their cup of caffeine and a little starchy sweet treat. Watching this perpetual lineup, I shook my head. A national coffee chain was actually doing a more reliable job of feeding everyone in a hospital than any food service operation was. That red cup and brown paper bag was in everyone's hands and peeked out of most of the patients' drawers. So, let's spend a bit of time talking about these corporate/franchise retail outlets.

It was fascinating for me to learn that generally speaking, food service franchisees in institutions are simply considered rent-paying vendors: the kind of food they're selling is essentially irrelevant. In many institutions, kitchens and dining halls were surrendered to franchises, who created food courts like you'd see in a shopping centre: a lineup of quick serve restaurants, many of them global chains offering some diversity in flavour, style, and price point. It's a pretty tidy way to take care of the need for on-site food service, and it's a low-risk move for the institution.

During my time at SickKids, I really felt the disconnection between the on-site food court and the hospital kitchen. While I was trying to promote organizational values around food service, with hard-earned buy-in from the institution, another part of that same institution was filling the space with exactly the kind of foods I was trying to eliminate. The lineup at Subway and Tim

Hortons always reminded me that *they* were the ones feeding the people in that space and my local food was not going to touch their popularity. No matter how much delicious, locally sourced, organic food I gave away for free, there was still going to be a lineup at Subway.

But if organizational values extended to food served on-site, institutions would have the power to make sure that the vendors complied with those core values. I giggled at the thought of asking Tim Hortons to purchase a certain minimum amount of their food ingredients from local sources or telling Booster Juice that they couldn't use Styrofoam cups because of our commitment to environmental sustainability. There is little to no precedent for something like this, and institutional administrators generally dance carefully around this issue, painfully hesitant to step on the toes of any corporate contract or relationship. These kinds of requests quickly slam up against operations mandates from these corporations. But if the Toronto Zoo can stop the McDonald's on its premises from using straws — because they were finding their way into the animal spaces and the animals were choking on them — then why can't every institution take a stand against global brands?

I've said before that a plate of food served anywhere reflects of the values and attitude that produced that plate, and the story institutions are telling is that serving contracts is the priority. We can't use a local supplier because they're not one of five suppliers who have been approved for use in all food service spaces. We can't change our third-party operator because they have a contract for 15 years. We can't say anything disparaging about Tim Hortons food because, somewhere, we've committed to that in a contract.

Many hospitals have a group purchasing organization, or GPO, that offers competitive, fixed pricing on certain items for a specific period of time for all members of the organization. For example, milk, or "liquid dairy" as it's known in these circles, could be sourced from a national supplier, and members of a GPO would commit to purchasing milk exclusively from this one supplier, which in turn offers a competitive price that is fixed for the duration of the purchasing contract. I was curious about the fine print on this contract, so I got my hands on a copy and read it carefully. I discovered that there was actually no penalty for buying outside of that particular group purchasing contract . . . but nobody knew this. Nobody had questioned it before.

One of the largest group purchasing organizations in Ontario is St. Joseph's Health System GPO; based in Brantford, just west of Toronto, they serve a wide variety of public institutions across Ontario. What I love about this GPO is that they've built it on values that prioritize local food, sustainability, and the resiliency of our local food system. This opens up access to institutional markets for small-scale farmers and producers in a way that previous GPOs did not. Up until the advent of this GPO, centralized purchasing was locked in with the industrial food system, and there was no practical way for smaller, regional suppliers to compete. But if you shift the values of the GPO itself, it opens up so much opportunity for like-minded vendors to access a market and for institutions to get more locally produced food. We know that most contracts make exactly zero mention of where the food comes from or how it is produced. In the absence of any other requirement, the lowest price will always take priority. But if an institution, or group of institutions, asserts some organizational values about food, then it would be possible to revisit contracts and make changes. There would be leverage to say that the highly processed, imported food does not comply with organizational values or that the institution's commitment to sustainability requires specific types of waste management. That kind of policy change would mean a huge win, but it would require institutions to shift their focus from legal contracts back to the social contract that we have with each other as humans.

So, did it stick? Has the change you made lasted? It's a question I get a lot, and it's a fair one. Well, the short answer is no. In something as complex as an institution, you need time and resources to make lasting change. I only seem to get about 12 months' worth of funding to evaluate the existing system; research and develop new processes; rework production, purchasing, and service; and implement the necessary communications strategies, both internally and externally. It takes about six months to really just understand the system. Let's not forget it's taken us about 30 years to get into this mess, and it's going to take longer than 12 months to get out of it. I leave before the glue is dry and we've confirmed that the new foundation is solid. But that's doesn't mean that the plan isn't good or won't work.

One of the most profound lessons I learned was that changing the food on the plates was actually only a small part of the challenge of this kind of project. What is more important is changing the governing ethos around food in the entire organization. You can quite easily plug in some new recipes, but if that change is not supported from the core and reflected everywhere in the institution, its chances of becoming permanent are quite low. If we are sincere about wanting the final outcome to change for patients, then our system needs to be fundamentally different going forward.

We also need to lift our gaze from the bottom line. While I was working at The Scarbrough Hospital, the most common question I was asked was if I'd figured out how to bring in local, scratch-made food in a way that's cheaper than what it currently costs to feed patients. While I fully understand that cost is a huge priority for hospitals, we cannot allow cost to be the guiding value for the food we serve. There *are* many ways to make locally sourced, scratch-made food cost-effective — remember that beautiful local turkey dinner added only $0.33 per patient — but what is really required here is a shift in our attitude. Constantly putting the lowest cost as the highest priority for patient food is precisely what got us into this wasteful mess, and we all have to acknowledge the fact that the way through requires some fundamentally different ideas about the role of food in nurturing good health and wellness.

With these hospital projects, I clearly pushed beyond the initial funding goals of putting more local food on institutional plates. I was convinced that a non-existent food culture was one of the most substantial barriers to making change, and I focused my efforts around rebuilding institutional food culture. One of the biggest lessons was that there's still so much more that we need to do, and that there are allies doing this good work in hospitals all over the world. After having many conversations with these folks over the years, I can tell you that their results are inspiring and encouraging. For instance, Health Care without Harm Europe has focused on food waste in hospitals and has profiled 10 European hospitals focusing on both what's going on patient trays and what's not being eaten by patients. They're employing diverse improvement strategies like scratch cooking, creating different portion sizes, using local organically grown ingredients, offering patients more choice on menus, employing host staff to take patient orders, flexible meal times, and serving meals that are enticingly plated, even on real china! The hospitality and sustainability in these projects is abundantly clear and they're getting results: 92 percent of patients in the Centre Hospitalier in Le Mans, France, were satisfied or very satisfied with their stay.

And as satisfaction scores have increased, food waste has decreased dramatically too. The University Hospital Complex of Santiago de Compostela served 2.6 million meals in 2015 and had a food waste rate of only 2.5 percent. In North America, the team at the UC San Francisco Medical Center addressed one very common barrier to patient eating: prescribed mealtimes for all patients. Once they switched their meal service to an on-demand model, where patients order food when they're hungry, their food waste fell by 30 percent. Ottawa's Children's Hospital of Eastern Ontario introduced a room service model for its patients in 2004 and broadened the cultural diversity of their menu offerings as well. These two elements combined have driven patient meal satisfaction scores from 30 percent to 98 percent while simultaneously lowering expenses and food waste, as the food that is served is actually getting eaten. Two hospitals in Haida Gwaii, British Columbia, and one hospital in Sioux Lookout, Ontario, have even created a way to serve traditional foods like wild fish, game, poultry, berries, herbs, and grains to their Indigenous patient population. Kathy Loon, the Miichim traditional food program coordinator at the Meno Ya Win Health Centre in Sioux Lookout, says, "We feel that serving traditional or Miichim food to patients is important culturally, spiritually, and nutritionally."

Canada is also home to Nourish Health Care. Founded by the McConnell Foundation, Nourish is the first-ever cohort of hospital food service administrators to work on reprioritizing the role of food in hospitals and patient care in Canada. Their connection with each other allows them to share best practices and work through challenges collaboratively. What I love about Nourish is that they've taken a beautifully holistic approach to addressing the rebuild of hospital food systems, including patient outcomes, mitigating the climate crisis, acknowledging Indigenous history and tradition, and making the best use of the $4 billion that is spent annually on hospital food in Canada. Plus, they're doing it in a way that addresses the diversity and nuance of Canadian communities. In fact, the great Leslie Carson is part of this cohort, representing a kitchen up north in the Yukon.

I've constantly been on the lookout for any hospital cooking their own meals. In this low-budget context, we can confidently say that any hospital in the country cooking food from scratch is doing so because of a conscious choice, one they've had to work hard to create and maintain. These are my allies in the trenches. Enter the Queensway Carleton Hospital in Ottawa, where meals are freshly prepared on-site, using as much of the local harvest as possible. There is lots of care and attention put into these meals, and there's no escaping the fact that this style of service costs more to deliver. The hospital's CFO and VP of corporate services, Carolyn Brennan, noted, "What ends up costing a little bit more on the staffing side is offset by the reduced waste."

Across the ocean in Denmark, the Gentofte Hospital in Copenhagen has taken some incredible leadership by preparing scratch-made food using locally grown, organic ingredients for both patients and staff in the hospital. To my delight, they've even created a snack cart that is wheeled around to patients, offering wholesome, delicious snacks to patients twice a day! Denmark has offered both mastery and trendsetting innovation in fine-dining restaurants, and it's wonderful to see those same values being applied to food service in hospitals.

Early on in my first hospital project, I noted the similarity between the words *hospital* and *hospitality*. This is not an obvious linguistic connection, and I was curious about what the roots were here. When I looked it up, I found that the word *hospital* comes from the Latin root *hospes*, which means stranger. The earliest manifestation of a hospital was a sort of public guest house, where strangers could arrive at the door and be welcomed in warmly. They were assessed on arrival and fed a meal that would restore their health and respond to whatever condition was detected. Medical care would sometimes follow, but food was always the first approach. Generations later, these early hospitals were taken over by the religious community and then the medical community, and the focus shifted from food to medicine as part of the first response. But the original point of hospitals was to be a place where anyone was welcomed and was offered food, rest, and comfort before they were sent out on their way. A hospital was once the place you went to receive hospitality! The irony that hospitality is the thing that has been slashed from hospital food service is undeniable. But I also see a huge opportunity, with the legacy of an existing history and tradition just waiting for us to step back into it. As with the hospital menus themselves, it seems we can find our way forward by looking at the things we've left behind.

CHAPTER 4

COLLEGES AND UNIVERSITIES

Feeding Minds with Good Food Culture

"The main educator of a child's palate in today's world may no longer be a parent but a series of multinational food companies."
— BEE WILSON, FOOD WRITER AND HISTORIAN

In the spring of 2013, students at Toronto's Ryerson University occupied the president's office. The complaint? Campus food: the price, the quality, and the lack of transparency in selecting third-party operators. On the front page of the *Toronto Star*, two students angrily held up two plates of lacklustre campus food: one included a wrap sandwich, with limp vegetables, meat, and a miscellaneous white sauce splashed about, and the other was a dry, defeated turkey and cheese sandwich on processed sliced bread. Although there are perhaps some nicer ingredients and better flavour in this food than what we've seen in hospitals, the story of this food is the same: highly processed ingredients assembled with the least amount of labour possible. When you take this approach to cooking, there's a real ceiling to how good any of it food can be, and this campus's food was the proof. "Pizza and wraps just don't cut it," said one student, and those ones certainly didn't. I was delighted at this loud student engagement, and had I been a student at the time, I would have been right there with them, fist in the air.

When I arrived on campus at McMaster University in my first year, the residence team handed me a frosh kit, full of everything I needed to get settled in: a roommate questionnaire, plastic mug, whistle, and sunscreen, plus a box of dried macaroni and cheese and two packets of ramen noodles. It took a second for me to realize that as a university student, this was now the kind of food I was going to eat. It was cheap, reasonably tasty, it filled you up, and nothing else really mattered. The "starving student" has somehow become a sort of charming archetype. But why do we glorify food insecurity and make jokes about the "Freshman 15"? At a time in their lives when they need their brains to handle more than ever before, we fill students with empty calories from cheap, processed food. A 2011 study of student eating habits in the *Journal of Nutrition Education and Behaviour* found that on average students weren't getting even a single daily serving of fruits and vegetables. We serve toddlers açai smoothies and homemade baby food, but when they're 17, we don't seem to mind when their diet consists of mostly mass-produced variations of starch. Those brains and bodies are still growing, so why aren't we focused on giving them what they need to thrive?

When we settle for "good enough" campus food, we completely miss the opportunity to use food service to support students. I think of it as a continuum. To the left, in the negative, is the status quo for most institutional food. We're getting by, making it work, and doing our best with what we've got. It's a bare bones operation almost exclusively focused on selling food to students or putting nutritionally adequate food on hospital patient trays. There are no extras, and everyone is prepared to learn to make do with less. We spend so much time here that we never see what's possible to the right, on the positive side of things. This is where we actually use food service to support the values and mandate of the institution. What does this mean? Just as the food served in hospitals and long-term care facilities should support healing and wellness, the food we serve in schools should somehow support academic excellence, and the food in prisons should, in some way, support rehabilitation.

What does this look like? Supporting academic excellence is about really understanding students and what's happening in their lives. It's having food available during the hours that students are hungry. It's about affordable, delicious, inclusive, accessible, and diverse menus. It's putting immuno boosts and comfort foods on the menus during exam season, and it's offering fun, engaging programming that makes life on campus feel a bit more nourishing and connected. It's making food *part* of their education, with informative signage, engaging programming, and on-campus gardens. This is an opportunity to create a culture of food that supports the learning and achievement that we should see in every one of our schools, colleges, and universities.

Shortly after the *Toronto Star* article had been published, Julia Hanigsberg, then vice president of administration at Ryerson University, reached out to me. She had heard about my work in hospitals and was curious about the crossover from health care to educational institutions. I had lots of ideas for how they could handle the demands of the dissatisfied students and chart a better way forward. Julia and I clicked instantly, and I was delighted to talk to an institutional administrator who actually valued the kind of food service and culture that I was advocating for. It became very clear that we were a good fit, and just a few months later, I accepted the position as Ryerson's assistant director of food services and executive chef. One major difference between hospitals and schools is the participation of the community in the system. At hospitals, it's more passive — the meal you get is the meal you get — but at schools, there's choice involved. I soon realized that my work at Ryerson would mean an education for me too.

My first day of work at Ryerson was residence move-in day. We ushered in more than 800 students and their loved ones, and once everyone was moved in and had said goodbye to their families, we served a welcome BBQ. This was quite literally the students' first taste of life at Ryerson. I didn't have any input on the meal and just jumped in to help serve the food: hamburgers and hot dogs grilled on the BBQ, potato salad, pasta salad, bean salad, Caesar salad, cookies, chips, and cans of pop. Watching the buffet lineup, I noticed the students were not choosing to take any of the salads. I decided to start serving the bean salad (arguably the most wholesome thing on the table) to see what kind of reception I would get. Some students were into it, others pulled their plates away, and others just walked right by. I decided to get a bit louder with my "cheerful" banter, talking about how their bodies needed more than meat and starch to keep going and that the sooner they made friends with fibre, the better. Some of those students would take some Caesar salad and point to it as evidence that they had succumbed to my vegetable pressure. I told them that what they had was lettuce covered in mayo and that it didn't count.

That day, I learned some really important things about the group of students I was about to feed. While I was trying to push salad, at least five students looked at me incredulously, saying, "I thought I had just said goodbye to my mother!" For most first-year students, this is their first taste of true independence. And for many of them, it's the first time they're making any real decisions about what they're going to eat. They are also arriving with the very natural desire to push back on whatever the culture of food was in their homes. Some choose to eat sugary cereals, others eat ice cream for dinner, and others eat poutine three meals a day. I remembered my own very similar rebellion when I was living in residence at university, and I realized that I needed to include this experience in the way we talk about food with first-year students. I was not going to get buy-in from students for my local, sustainably sourced wholesome food by dismissing where they were.

When I'd talk to groups of students to introduce them to Ryerson Eats (the new name for campus food service), I would tell them that we were there to take care of them and make sure that the food was more wholesome and nutritious but also super delicious. I would go a bit further and tell them that they were about to take more control over what they ate and be more responsible for keeping the machine that is their body in good working order. I'd encourage them to go out there and enjoy themselves, experiment with newfound freedom — eat poutine for breakfast — and see how it all feels. But then I'd tell them that in about three months, when their bodies start to scream at them, I would be there with delicious tasting food that was also good for their bodies. I'd urge them not to let a power struggle with their parents define their personal relationship with food and I'd tell them that eating is a habit they'll have for the rest of their lives, so they should consider working on their relationship with food and laying down a solid foundation. I'd remind them that I wanted to help them meet and surpass all of their goals and dreams, but they'd have to decide on how to fuel that journey. Eventually they'd start asking more questions, and I'd take all the time required to answer every one.

One time, I was speaking with a group of students who were all among the first generation in their families to attend post-secondary school. I was there to talk to those students about the new face of food services and how we made decisions about what to serve to students. I wanted to inspire them to care about what they ate, beyond how delicious it was or how much it cost. I wanted them to care about their community and the long line of people involved in getting their food to them. What I learned from them was that many first-generation students don't have the emotional or financial support of their families and have to figure out how to pay for their university education themselves. When they graduate, they carry an average debt of $16,727 for Canadian university students or $28,650 for Americans. The financial load is heavy enough, but the lack of emotional support was something I hadn't considered. I thought back to my own time at university, and there was never any question about my parents letting me bring all of my laundry home, taking me to the grocery store before dropping me back off at school, and sliding me every little bit of extra money they could. In fact, it was how I made it through university, and I couldn't imagine having done it without my parents' support, both financially and emotionally. And when your plate is this full, who has time to give a shit about how that egg was raised or where that fruit came from? If you can barely pay your rent, are you going to spend extra money on a grass-fed burger? Hell no. I get it. Every one of these conversations with students further reminded me that students are a population essentially on a fixed income, much like senior citizens and people on social assistance and disability support. And while there are legitimate arguments in favour of spending more on our food than we currently do, students don't have the luxury of spending more for better quality food. The money they were currently spending each day for food on campus should have been able to feed them well. What they really needed was better value and a better experience from what they were already spending, and it was my job to figure out how to deliver that.

When I arrived in August 2013, Ryerson was in its final months of a 20-year contract with Aramark, one of the world's largest third-party operators. These corporations deliver food services to institutions like schools, hospitals, prisons, and long-term care facilities; in public spaces like stadiums, arenas, airports, museums, and galleries; and in remote areas like mining camps and cruise ships. Generally speaking, the contracts are either a profit-and-loss contract, where the operator takes ownership of the entire food service operation, or a management fee contract, where the institution pays the operator a set fee to manage their food service. For institutions, it's hands-off, turn-key service. Aramark's size and scope allows them to cultivate purchasing relationships with certain suppliers offering competitive pricing and a variety of other benefits. There are, however, some pretty sharp criticisms of food service operators: with profit being their priority, they serve low-quality, highly processed food at high prices, use opaque contracts that favour corporate brands, and have little to no connection to the campus community.

I think that the great strength of a third-party operator is their delivery of logistics and capacity. Their ability to deploy a team to produce huge volumes of food is unparalleled. They can get an operation up and running effectively and efficiently, even in the most remote and unusual locations. Operators come with a network of suppliers and contractors, and for an administrator who does not want to deal with the hassle of managing a self-operated food service, they really are an easy solution. They value standardization and consistency, and their models can be widely distributed and replicated with little adjustment. They are not visionaries or thought leaders, nor should they be. The visioning is the responsibility of the institution, *not* the third-party operator.

Now, it's perhaps fair to mention that when many institutions were being established and values were being set, the industrial food system was an unknown possibility and nobody imagined that food would need to be protected. But now here we are, with an incredibly vulnerable food system and institutional food service that is quite famously ridiculed. I know it may feel like a huge investment to generate and articulate organizational values around food, but the truth is these values already exist, they're just not being applied to the food service.

What I am asking for here is a more holistic and authentic assertion of institutional values.

Considering the loud objections Ryerson was receiving from students about the existing operator's service, it made sense that they were considering switching campus food services to a self-operated model, to move the responsibility and production in-house. I would have happily advocated for and assisted with this, but there were two compelling reasons for us to embrace the idea of putting out a request for proposals (RFP) for another operator: first, there was not enough time between the end of their existing contract and the start of the academic year in September to make the switch to a self-op model and be up and running to receive students. The move to self-op requires much larger-scale change than we could pull off in only a few months. Second, the vast majority of campuses in the country have a third-party operator, and in the interest of making change that is relevant and applicable to other campuses, it seemed worthwhile to invest in a new model that included them in the story. I pitched Ryerson the idea of asserting their own vision for campus food service. I encouraged them to consider and articulate how they wanted people to engage with food on campus and then ask the operators to play along. I worked with an evaluation and selection committee that included administration, faculty, and students as decision-makers, and me as an industry expert, and together we crafted a vision for campus food services that reflected Ryerson's values while also addressing the complaints and demands of the students. I pushed them on setting more ambitious goals for local procurement and on articulating local, sustainably produced food as the most desirable. We discussed the importance of reflecting the diversity of the Ryerson community in our menus while also reflecting the seasons and celebrating local suppliers. The students wanted affordable pricing, extended hours for hot meal service on campus, and more transparency with the process. We also included a waste mitigation and management component and required a commitment to invest in compelling programming to engage students in food issues. We were asking a lot, and if nobody responded to our RFP, we'd know that we had overshot.

Ultimately, the three largest operators on the planet submitted proposals, and that told us that operators were ready to get on board. We couldn't yet measure their sincerity and commitment to new values, but it was a promising sign. The committee selected Chartwells, the education arm of Compass Group Canada, the world's largest third-party food service operator. They came to the table ready to play and excited about making some changes to the national landscape of campus food service. As part of the new promise we were making to students, I was to be the campus's seat of accountability for the food services contract. My job was to rebuild the culture of food on campus, and working closely with the operator was a huge part of that. Say what you want about corporate food service folks being exclusively focused on profit, the Chartwells/Compass team jumped in on a model that is quite different from anything they were used to doing, and they agreed to let me steer the ship. At our expectations meeting, I was upfront about the fact that this was going to be harder for Chartwells because they had to deal with me. It was going to be messy and often frustrating, and they would surely find themselves wondering why they agreed to this in the first place, but I also promised that we'd build something that was solid and honestly successful, in a way that could hopefully be replicated on other campuses.

One of the issues that Ryerson students had raised was about the opacity of the contracts — the only versions they'd been able to see had redacted information. When we finalized the contract between Ryerson and Chartwells, one of the stipulations was that we would agree to provide a completely clean, unredacted copy of the contract to the student union, a big ask for both Ryerson and Chartwells. This was not something that happened frequently or easily, but after a sign-off from both legal teams, I was given a clean copy of the contract, which we very happily delivered to the student union leadership. To me, this was a very big deal, and I was grateful to both Ryerson and Chartwells for cooperating. The student union could see exactly what was being asked for, the fees that were being paid, and all of the fine print. Equity, sustainability, and justice were things that student government and the students themselves were loudly demanding, and we were building a version of campus food services that gave them the values-driven food service they were seeking. But we also needed to repair a relationship with the students and the student union. We had to rebuild trust, and I worked hard at being as visible, open, and accountable as possible. One of our biggest early wins was being named one of the Ryerson Student Union's Partners of the Year in 2014. We still had a long way to go, but this let us know that we were on the right track.

Ryerson's campus had two residences, each with its own kitchen and dining room, serving over 850 students three meals day. Meal plans were mandatory for residence students, but essentially all our food service was an à la carte retail offering. We had one big café on campus with full breakfast and lunch service, a café in the athletic centre, about seven Tim Hortons coffee outlets that also served our to-go food, and a busy catering business that supported events across the campus seven days a week. All told, our retail food service produced about 3,500 meals a day.

Part of the change that the students (and I) wanted to see on the menu was better food that accommodated dietary concerns and was still affordable. We had three major menus to build, in the main café and in each of the two residences. We decided to do a two-week rotation to offer lots of variety and diversity on the menu. Of course, there's always talk that the mandate of institutional menus is to provide healthy meals. But what does that really mean in this context? I remembered considering this very same thing during my time at The Stop. Generally, our conventional understanding of healthy food involves low levels of fat and salt and higher levels of fibre and protein. This message is usually delivered by someone in a white coat, wagging their finger. There's no talk about the flavour or pleasure involved in the food or any mention of how or where the thing was grown. So, I took a cue from my past self and brought forward that same philosophy of wholesome, affordable, delicious food for our campus menus.

It's no surprise that scratch cooking is at the top of my list for the way forward for institutional food. The Chartwells team knew that this was a big priority for me, and they worked hard at building menus that found efficient ways to use labour to make this happen. Of course, this meant that our spending on labour had to be watched diligently, as the numbers could and did spike quite easily. I was totally okay with a pared-down menu and simplified food if it meant we were able to take care of all of our production in-house.

Rossy Earle, an accomplished chef from the restaurant, retail, and catering worlds, was our retail chef manager and looked after all the meals served at our main location on campus. She was committed to our new food values and is really good at figuring out how to make things work. Rossy is a brilliant cook all around, but there's something extra special that happens with her soups and sauces. After a renovation in our main café on campus, we built a station offering six different soups each day, all made from scratch on-site by Chef Rossy. In accordance with our new values around inclusion, all dietary restrictions were provided for here, and word about the delicious soups got out quite quickly. We started posting daily menus on our social media feed each morning, and sometimes during peak hours, there was even a lineup at the (self-serve) soup station! Rossy enjoyed some celebrity status on campus, and I was delighted that everyone was eating so much wholesome, good food.

Scratch cooking made better food, but it did challenge some conventions. For example, Chartwells had a program that provided students with printouts of the nutritional information for each dish on our menu — a popular feature on other campuses. I firmly refused to participate. The biggest reason was because it clipped the wings of our chefs. In order to provide that nutritional printout, a reliable recipe needs to be entered into a software program, which does the calculations. But if the kitchen team is working efficiently, they adapt their recipes based on what needs to be used or what there's a bumper crop of; there is no time to write, test, and enter a recipe into a software program before service on the chance that someone will want the information that day. To me, that time and effort was better spent actually cooking. Besides, I would tell students that this numbers-based approach to understanding their food wasn't really that effective, and if they wanted to see some healthy change, they should spend a week not eating anything that comes in a package. I surprisingly got no strong pushback on my decision, and some students even took up the package-free challenge and reported an eye-opening experience!

We had two restaurant franchises on campus, one serving pizza and the other serving wraps. Ryerson ran these outlets in strict accordance with each corporation's production guidelines. We had the benefit of a recognizable, popular quick-serve restaurant chain, but we were limited by their purchasing structure, policies, and procedures. I was irritated that we had to continue purchasing industrial ingredients to prepare that food. Here's where having an organizational mandate and mission statement that is applied to food service offers power and leverage. In the interest of being as fair as possible, I asked those vendors about their sourcing, and if they would consider more wholesome, sustainable food ingredients. It's no surprise that they were not able to provide any details on their sourcing, but it was important to walk through this process. As it became clear that this particular food service was no longer in line with the vision we had for our campus food offerings, our values allowed us to end those contracts. Yes, it's difficult to end a lengthy relationship, and sometimes you're locked into a contract and may have to wait it out, but this was a pretty simple move to make. We created our own pizza production and a build-your-own salad and sandwich station, which allowed us to serve the food we wanted to serve without a corporate brand looming above. There's no question that the institution is a behemoth of bureaucracy, and making change is usually messy and complicated. But sometimes, making change is actually quite simple and easy; you just have to ask for it.

Diversifying our food options was another must, since Toronto boasts one of the most diverse populations on the planet. Every day for lunch and dinner there was a hot entrée, like baked pasta, aloo gobi, or moussaka. But the aloo gobi wasn't just there for the Indian students; everyone can get down with a delicious curry, just like everyone can enjoy Korean short ribs or fish and chips. I did not want these diverse flavours showing up exclusively on some kind of "ethnic food night" menu. For us, diversity needed to be regular and mainstream. Similarly, there were always vegan and vegetarian options available that were thoughtfully created. Having menus that meet students where they are is about inclusion and hospitality. It tells students that we see them, and we understand what they're asking for. And honestly, this was not hard. Sometimes it was as simple as offering beans as an alternative to bacon or sausage in our all-day breakfast. We narrowed menu items, but we made almost everything ourselves. The hallways around our cafés would smell mouth-wateringly promising before lunchtime, and it was wonderful to see people getting excited about the food and racing over because there was African peanut soup that day or pies fresh out of the oven. Nothing helps draw people in like enticing them to follow their noses.

Now, I can't talk about all of our delicious in-house production without talking about its impact on labour. There is no question that scratch cooking requires more labour — it's precisely those human hands that we want — but we had to be very careful about not letting labour costs balloon. I was really pushing for our team to produce everything we sold, but for a number of legitimate reasons — like the available skill of our team, the available labour hours for production, and the amount of kitchen space and appliances — there were limits on what we could produce in-house. Part of my insistence on in-house production was about wanting to serve food that did not contain the fillers, flavour enhancers, and additives that you often find in pre-packaged food, and I was skeptical about a supplier's ability to provide us with food that fit our new values. Thankfully, I was totally wrong about these assumptions! We decided to start by bringing in baked goods we didn't have the capacity to produce ourselves and that weren't contractually relegated to Tim Hortons' production, as with doughnuts and muffins. I reached out to a few vendors and explained what we were looking for, and the majority of producers were delighted to be a part of our new food story on campus. We had frozen croissants from The Tempered Room, a beautiful French-inspired café run by Bertrand Alépée, that baked into buttery, flaky pillows from heaven. We also ordered frozen scones from Sandra Katsiou at Baker and Scone, and when we baked them freshly each morning, the whole ground floor of the building smelled like rich, buttery, pastry goodness.

After the success of our baked goods outsourcing, we decided to try burgers. I would have loved to have ground and formed all of those burger patties in-house, but we just didn't have the available staff or space to do it. But something really interesting happened with VG Meats, our awesome beef supplier, who made their own burgers. Yes, they were frozen burgers, but they were frozen burgers made without any weird fillers and using good, naturally raised local beef. In the last year of my time at Ryerson, meat prices had surged, and restaurants and food service outlets were all feeling the pinch. We considered shrinking the size of our burger, but after testing it out, we realized that it altered the patty-to-filling ratio in a way that was not enjoyable, and we wanted to keep prices as accessible as possible. Thankfully, the fine folks at VG Meats had a solution. They had recently partnered with a mushroom farmer who had a significant surplus of portobello mushroom stems that he was just throwing away. Adding an ounce of mushrooms to a smaller quantity of beef allowed us to maintain the size of our patty, but with the very complementary meaty flavour and texture of portobello mushrooms. The mushrooms were almost undetectable and added a juicy umami flavour to the burger, while also encouraging a bit more plant-forward eating. We put up a sign explaining what we had done at the grill station, and the students, staff, and faculty literally ate it up.

Thankfully, my outsourcing investigations uncovered an amazing opportunity for us to broaden our community of suppliers with shared values, support local business and agriculture, and get some of the best food in the province onto our campus menus.

The most important goal of this whole project was to earn back the trust and patronage of the students, and so it was crucially important that the frontline staff could readily explain the changes we were making. If you say that you serve local food, but none of your staff can offer any information on where the ingredients come from, you are not taking this seriously. If you say that you will accommodate celiac students in the residence dining hall, the staff members they engage with every day should be well versed in the procedure, with separate toasters, knives, and cutting boards. And, of course, if you're promoting new, delicious food, the team needs to be able to answer questions and talk about how things taste.

Communications in general are often dismissed and devalued, and I think internal communication is precisely where so much change-making falls apart. In order to do this well, we invested pretty heavily in staff training and development. We took the staff to farms to see where some of the produce we were serving was grown. We brought vendors in during staff meetings and did tastings of new items as they were introduced, and we would put promotional materials and signage up on the walls in the kitchen to communicate messaging about sourcing and seasonality to the team. I also led a couple of training sessions with our whole staff about some of the bigger picture stuff: What is sustainability? Why do we care about local sourcing? What is so great about free-run eggs? All of this training and engagement was supported by a daily pre-service meeting where staff and management in the main kitchen and two residences would gather each morning to talk about the day ahead. This was a perfect place to share information about seasonal promotions, harvest notes from farms, and our support strategy to get students through exam time. I cannot stress enough the importance of investing time and effort into an internal communications strategy for your team. This is where the execution of your organizational values really counts. My gauge for measuring an organization's success in making change or asserting new values is the level of competency and interest of the frontline staff. If your grassroots service team doesn't know and can't talk about the change you say you're making, you are not making that change. It is as simple as that.

Our communication went beyond students too: we knew there were a lot of parents worrying about their children out in the world for the first time. Every year on move-in day, Ryerson Student Affairs holds an info session for the parents and guardians who have just dropped off a student in residence. One year, Brandon Smith, the manager of residence life and education with Student Affairs, invited me to tell students and parents all about the new, fresh face of campus food services.

I talked about local sourcing, with photos of the farm where our root vegetables were coming from on the screen behind me. I told them about our commitment to scratch cooking, cultural diversity, and balanced eating, with lots of interesting options for vegans, vegetarians, and students with gluten and dairy intolerances. I saw the anxiety in some mothers' eyes before I assured them that we always had halal options. In fact, during our second year, we decided that all of the chicken served on campus would be halal. That way no one had to sort out which location was serving halal meat, making things easy and consistent for Muslim students and for our own ordering process.

It felt wonderful to introduce parents to the food service that we had built and to let them know that we were working really hard to take very good care of their kids. I answered every single question, held every worried mom's hand, and explained the process for telling the residence food team about a student's dietary restriction. Some of those parents were farmers themselves who knew the farms we had partnered with. My presentation slides on sourcing got a round of applause! My confident presentation of the systems that were already in place to keep gluten-free eaters safe and to make sure that there was always a hot meal for vegans sent a message to students and their families that we were on it.

And from a leadership perspective, I really believe that it's better to investigate what your community needs and provide it, rather than waiting for your constituency to come begging or banging on your door. We knew that dietary restrictions were an important consideration for students, so we met them where they were. We knew our job wasn't just to provide food but to provide comfort, safety, and a sense of care, so that even though they've left their families behind, students still had plenty of people in their corner.

Of course, real change requires a purchasing structure that works and reflects your organizational values. In North America the majority of hospitals and post-secondary schools use a third-party operator for their food service, which means that all purchasing goes through the books of the operators, who in turn cultivate relationships with producers and suppliers. With third-party operators, the savings come to institutions via rebates, where a percentage of the spend with specific suppliers is returned to the institution at the end of a given fiscal cycle as a sort of bonus reward. Third-party operators dangle these rebates as part of their pitch to schools, and many post-secondary institutions rely on these rebates to keep daily operations running. With all respect to operators and this system, this rebate-based approach to purchasing food only works in the context of the industrial food system and is otherwise fundamentally unsustainable. On the ground, we often see elevated original pricing, meaning the institution actually pays upfront for its rebate, and they play a silly pass-the-money game with suppliers so everyone feels like they've gotten a good deal. To make matters worse, this rebate is often built on the backs of the producers themselves, as they drop unit pricing in favour of volume sales. For large corporations with national and international distribution, this can be an effective and affordable strategy to growing business, but for a small family farm it does not work. The average annual salary for a Canadian farmer is $40,839, and what's more, they generally only have income for a few months each year, making rebated pricing completely untenable. The idea of asking a farmer to return a portion of the money that was spent over the course of the year to a customer is quite simply ridiculous.

One of my stipulations for purchasing through Chartwells was that I would bring my own suppliers to the table, and 100km Foods was the first new vendor that I brought on board. Chartwells managed the books for food service, so all purchasing went through them, but they were willing to take on my new suppliers, who I knew shared our values about food and would be willing to invest in building a relationship with an institution. I was focused on paying them fairly and promptly for their food, hoping that the size and reliability of an institution's purchasing could help them sustain and grow their business while giving us access to wholesome, delicious, locally grown food.

While I maintain that we are more than the decisions we make with our wallets, procurement is vital. Having our values underpin our purchasing enabled us to implement this change right at the root, with the producers we chose to do business with. Up until this point, the right (read: lowest) price has generally been the sole guiding value for institutional food purchasing, when the truth is there is much more that we need to know about a producer and their product before placing an order. In the purchasing policy that I built at Ryerson, five questions guided our purchasing:

1. Is this the product we need (size, colour, flavour, etc.)?
2. How was this product grown (conventional, organic, or transitional)?
3. Where was this produced (distance to market)?
4. What kind of operation is producing this (small family farm, co-op, or large corporate farm)?
5. Is the price fair and affordable (market rate, within budget)?

In creating a values-based purchasing policy to guide our spending, I used the procurement toolkit from the Association for the Advancement of Sustainability in Higher Education (AASHE) as a starting point. AASHE suggested creating a matrix to position your most desirable purchasing sources in one quadrant and your least desirable sources in another other. For us, the ideal food purchasing scenario would be purchasing organically grown food from a local farm owned by a family. Conversely, the least desirable supplier would offer conventionally grown food from a corporate farm on another continent. Of that ideal trinity, the organically grown piece is often the hardest to fulfill due to challenges with pricing and availability. So, if I can't find or afford the organic food, can I find a small, local supplier who is transitioning their farm to an organic operation? Or can I start with locally grown, conventionally raised food from a family farm? Or perhaps there's a local, organic grower that is a small farm co-op? This process is certainly more time consuming and requires much more information from a vendor than has previously been asked. Let's face it, the convenience of the quick, one-stop shop from a central supplier is a big part of the obstacle to change. But my desire to use our purchasing to shrink the gap between producer and consumer, nurture local small business, support sustainable agriculture, and get the best quality food we could afford onto the campus was worth a little inconvenience.

I was really excited to bring in some better quality food and support local producers who could often do a better job of meeting our needs, both with the food they were producing and the values that they brought to the table. For example, the catering team at Ryerson produced lots of sweets platters for meetings and receptions on campus. At the time, most of those sweets were brought in frozen and either thawed to serve or baked on-site. We purchased cookies through our dry goods supplier that were baked in an oven that came from the vendor as part of the sales pitch. For whatever reason, these cookies were chronically undercooked (I suspect to suggest that they were chewy). They did not taste very good, and we would often see people breaking them in half, not wanting to eat the entire four-inch cookie. The thing is, nobody will pick up a half cookie from a platter, so that bit always ended up as waste. I reached out to the company to see if they had or could make smaller cookies for us. After getting passed around on the phone, I spoke with someone who said that there's no way they could make a different size cookie, as their machine was only designed to produce that one size. Right, of course. I made inquiries with a couple of other vendors in our supplier's inventory, and nobody was able or willing to offer me a smaller cookie.

This seemed ridiculous, so I got in touch with Andrea Mut, who had a bakery here in Toronto, not far from the Ryerson campus. I asked her if she could make us a three-inch cookie with good ingredients for the same price we were paying for the cookies from Sysco. She arrived the next day with five cookie samples, one of which was gluten-free and all of which were crazy delicious. Our first order of cookies was for 500 pieces, and that quickly became our weekly requirement. The cookies were a big hit, and we never had leftovers or waste, as people would stuff them into their pockets for later. Andrea was using chocolate from ChocoSol,

a local social enterprise producing fairly traded, artisanal chocolate, who reached out to me with thanks for
the bump they saw in their sales as a result of our order
with Andrea. Andrea's cheesecake made with Monforte
Dairy's chèvre quickly made its way to our catering
menu, and her legendary butter tarts would sell out in
our retail cafés daily. A local paper did a story about us,
celebrating a public institution supporting local small
business and exclaiming that it was a win-win situation
all around. Sheldon Levy, then university president,
sent me a huge thank you when he saw the article. He
was delighted that he could finally speak publicly about
campus food again and that Ryerson was a part of this
kind of local innovative impact. And speaking of the
president, on the occasions that he'd surprise us with a
last-minute request for a dinner, Andrea would speed
over with two of his favourite desserts to help us make
it happen.

During convocation in June, we had a series of
receptions for graduating students and their families
over the course of a couple of weeks. The food service
was tea, coffee, lemonade, and sweets, and we ordered
a total of 16,000 cookies from Andrea for these receptions. On her Instagram feed, she posted photos of the
all-hands-on-deck cookie dough rolling happening in
her kitchen. She had her son and her son's girlfriend in
on it too! With the increased business, Andrea was able
to buy equipment to scale up her business, hire staff, and
even take a vacation. Nobody from Sysco was bothered

about this loss of cookie sales, but our decision to purchase more thoughtfully and in accordance with our values actually changed people's lives with a ripple of growth and positivity.

Sometimes beautiful local food was a bit outside our budget, but we could still find creative partnerships that benefitted everyone. Bryan Gilvesy naturally raises Texas Longhorn cattle in Tillsonburg, Ontario, producing 100 percent grass-fed beef. Unfortunately, it was more expensive than we could afford for our retail operation, and I certainly was not expecting a discount on the back of the farmer. If we got a deal, we'd have to earn it and send something of equal value back in Bryan's direction. At the time, he sold almost exclusively to restaurants, and at the end of each month, he'd find himself with a bit of meat that hadn't sold and begrudged keeping it in the freezer and sitting on inventory. One month he called us, saying that he had beef cheeks and sirloin steaks and offered us a deal in the interest of moving the inventory. Now, we had freezer space and the ability to do something beautiful with that meat, so we took everything Bryan had. A few weeks later, we served a delicious beef cheek ravioli at a celebratory dinner held for one of our honorary doctorate degree recipients. Bryan got an empty fridge, and we got beautiful beef to serve our guests at a discount that was fair to everyone. To me, this is good business.

It is safe to say that in all of my institutional work, my largest and most unexpected lessons — and some of my biggest mistakes — came from managing the labour through this change. Working in an institutional kitchen means working with union labour, and I knew nothing about union culture or how to engage with union staff. I didn't understand how sacred collective agreements were, and I didn't realize that changes can't really happen quickly or without layers of discussion and approval. That said, my politics are, and will always be, pro-labour. I will always believe that people should make a living wage for a good day's work, that everyone should have access to the opportunity to work, and that there should be mechanisms in place that protect people's safety, health, and, to some extent, their quality of life. I want to revalue all the people involved in making food, and I want more people working in kitchens!

What I know now is that when I worked in hospitals, I should have been more explicit and deliberate about engaging union leadership right from the start. I should have clearly outlined the goals of the project and the hopeful plan for labour moving forward. The administration should have asked for their input on how we rolled the change out to the team, and we should have been more unified in our embrace of this change. Hearing that management was "reworking things" usually signals pink slips. The staff didn't know me at all, and they certainly didn't trust me. Change-making would have been much easier with the support of the union.

When I *did* reach out to the union, my hospital projects went much more smoothly. Early on, one of the staff at The Scarborough Hospital raised some concern about me working in the kitchen, and specifically that my hands could not make any food that was sent up to patients, because I would be essentially displacing union labour. There was no way I could run that project and support production of new menu items without occasionally participating in food prep. I reached out to union leadership to explain the situation, and thankfully, they gave me a green light to do whatever I needed to do in that kitchen for the purposes of training. In fact, they were so excited about this project that they wanted to find a way to document this process with a camera crew! I asked that they pass this communication through their internal channels, as it was very important that the team knew that this permission was legitimate and not just something I came up with after going out for lunch. I will remain forever grateful to my friends at the Canadian Union of Public Employees, who have been consistent allies of me and my work since those early days at the hospital.

As I started to make changes at Ryerson, I realized there was now a discrepancy between what we were asking the food service team to do and the expectations outlined in their job descriptions. We also had some hiring to do, and I really wanted to make sure that our new vision for food service was accurately described in the job postings. The same way the university prioritized equity, diversity, and inclusion, it also now valued sustainability, community, and accountability. I also couldn't ask anyone to do anything that wasn't in their job description, and constantly hitting that wall was becoming frustrating. Cooking from scratch was not part of their job descriptions, and neither was upholding the university's values around sustainability, and our management team would have challenges from staff about the new things they were being asked to do. So, with the Chartwells team and Ryerson HR, we took on the enormous task of reviewing and rewriting the entire department's job descriptions.

I wanted to prioritize cooking skills and assert our new departmental values about food, and from a change-making perspective, this was a groundbreaking move. Change is real when an employer starts asking different things of its employees. Existing staff would be supported through the transition to new job descriptions with training and professional development programming. This was a painstaking and complicated process, but we did it! We reviewed and made adjustments to every single job description in the department, which is something that hadn't happened in at least 10 years. We shared these changes with union leadership, and then we shared these descriptions with the staff, answered all of their questions, and made any necessary adjustments. After all of this, we had a situation where everyone in the department was on the same page about our new organizational values and feeling positive about the way forward. They understood what we meant by local sourcing and sustainability, and they knew what part of that they were responsible for executing. I don't know that anyone else was as excited about this, but to me this was a giant triumph. At the time, no other institutional food service department had sustainability and hospitality values mentioned in their job descriptions.

Here's an example of the change in action on our receiving team. Previously, ordering was very standardized, and more often than not, the receiving team placed orders that simply maintained steady levels of inventory. They were not required to make decisions about what to order, as that had already been determined by the chef or GM. Once orders arrived, one of our staff would take the invoice and make sure that everything listed had actually been delivered, and then the team would unpack the order. Before we started purchasing the bulk of our produce from 100km Foods, we were using the existing produce supplier, who told us that they could deliver local produce. One afternoon I was in the kitchen office and saw a sign on the wall above the receiver's desk that said "order Ontario apples only." I threw my arms in the air and did a victory dance! However, my insistence that the team order *only* Ontario apples and refuse Washington apples meant, from an HR perspective, that this employee now had some decision-making capacity around spending, which meant a pretty significant boost in the responsibility level of their job description. This is another example of how making one change in an institution requires a ripple of changes throughout the institution. Ultimately, the receivers ended up with a little salary increase, and you better believe that we never saw another Washington apple in that kitchen again.

It's important to note that little changes like this happened all the time in all three projects. Moving from standardized, industrial food to more whole, farm-fresh ingredients required our team to use their senses and good judgment more frequently. They had to maintain a proper rotation in the fridge and pay attention to things that might be spoiling. Not just ordering the same thing over and over again required the teams to pay a bit more attention to inventory and to communicate more thoroughly with the chef. Changes like these meant putting more human skills — and more humanity — back into the kitchen.

About a year into my time at Ryerson, I decided that it was time to bring production of packaged salads, sandwiches, yogurt parfaits, and fruit cups in-house. Up until this point, we had outsourced these items to a third party, which was doing a pretty mediocre job and couldn't tell us anything about the origin of any of the ingredients in those products. We already had a team of people in the basement kitchen who were making some of these things, and I presented Rossy with the challenge of figuring out how to pull this off, so that our to-go offerings were a proper reflection of our values.

For a busy campus full of people on the go, it was really important to have a menu of food that was wholesome, delicious, affordable, and easily available to grab on the way to a class or meeting. The status quo versions of these foods are largely tasteless and uninspired. The sandwich bread is soggy, the fruit is sour (because it's imported and out of season), and nothing feels like good value for money, but you choke it back because you're hungry and you've already bought the thing. Foods like these are often produced in large quantity in a centralized, commissary kitchen, then shipped out to many retail locations each morning. This was the original arrangement we had with a supplier brought to us by the Chartwells team. Aside from the fact that the food did not look or taste very good, I didn't like that someone else's branding was on the package and that the food didn't tell *our* story. There is a way to make a really good egg salad sandwich or a really delicious cup of veggies and dip, and I was convinced that with some thought and attention, we could pull it off.

Chef Rossy's task was to come up with the menu and its seasonal iterations, then find appropriately sized compostable packaging while making sure that all of the items remained affordable. Once we had the food in the package, we needed a label. Melissa Yu Vanti, our communications master, designed a beautiful graphic that conveyed our new vibe and vision, then painstakingly hunted down labels that could be composted as well.

Ultimately, we ended up with a really beautiful menu. We sourced whole-grain organic sandwich bread from Grainharvest Breadhouse, a bakery in Waterloo, and made egg- and tuna-salad sandwiches with scallions and parsley for brightness and crunch (and, of course, no dry corners!). Our yogurt parfaits were made with granola from Kimberley's Own, a small local supplier who was making a low-sugar, vegan, gluten-free granola that tasted really good, and Greek yogurt from the lovely people at Sheldon Creek Dairy that we sweetened with a touch of Rosewood honey. This was a beautiful thing and easily became one of our bestselling items. In fact, we went through so much yogurt that our friends at Sheldon Creek had trouble keeping up with our demand! People are often skeptical about the capacity of local producers to provide the volume required for something like institutional food services, but the truth is the capacity is definitely there. And having a local supplier who's not able to meet demand is one of the best problems to have! If we ever get to a point where there are not enough farmers to fulfill the requests of kitchens in public institutions, I will weep with joy!

The final steps in getting our in-house grab and go up and running was training the production team to prepare these foods. When Chef Rossy shared the news with the team, they were hesitant. They were used to making about 20 sandwiches daily, and now they needed to produce about 100 pieces of each menu item each day. Both Rossy and I were convinced that there was a way to do this with our existing labour force and that it was just a matter of teaching them some prep tricks to make the process more productive and efficient. When they had to make just 20 sandwiches, the team could afford to pick up each piece of bread, and methodically use the spreader to spread the egg salad, as though they were packing up for a family picnic. But at 100, a new approach was required. I remember peeping into the prep room when Rossy introduced the team to the wonders of an ice cream scoop. If they laid down 10 slices of bread, they could quickly pop a scoop of egg or tuna salad on each slice, then use their spreader to even things out. In a few short minutes, Rossy had 10 sandwiches made, and the team was in shock about how quickly that happened. They were excited and motivated, and they worked their butts off in that basement kitchen preparing sandwiches, pasta and quinoa salads, yogurt granola parfaits, crudité with dip, and in-season, fresh fruit cups with honey yogurt . . . all of which sold for under $5 each!

We got the most encouraging sign things were going well when one afternoon I was driving to an appointment and listening to *Here and Now*, hosted by Gill Deacon on CBC Radio. That afternoon, Gill was asking all of her guests what they had for lunch, and she was speaking with a lawyer who said that she had eaten lunch on the Ryerson campus. She'd grabbed an egg-salad sandwich and ate it en route to the CBC studio, not expecting very much, but she said the sandwich was delicious! I had been on Gill's show not long before that, talking about the changes we were making to the menu at Ryerson, so she knew the backstory and gave us all a really lovely shout-out on the very day we were working so hard to build the team's confidence about their ability to pull off this new challenge. I remember shaking my head in disbelief that this had actually happened while tears of deep gratitude rolled down my cheeks. I called Rossy from the car to tell her about it, and she started screaming and crying too. The next morning, she pulled the to-go production team into her office and played the podcast of the show for them, with much celebration and excitement. The team was nicely puffed up and excited when they returned to work. For me, it was a thumbs-up from the universe, a clear indicator that we were on the right track and should keep going for it.

Even with these new efficiencies and skill developments, our production team needed more help processing raw ingredients, and in the fall of 2014, we met the lovely people at the Hospitality Workers' Training Centre, located just a couple of blocks away from the Ryerson campus. The HWTC offers skills building training programs that enable un- and under-employed folks to find good jobs in the city's hospitality industry. Our values were clearly aligned, and in a conversation with the training centre, we uncovered a pretty cool opportunity. The trainees needed work and the chance to develop their skills, and we needed our locally sourced, raw vegetables to be processed and chopped to the specs required by our menus. We connected Chef Rossy from our kitchen with Chef Ricky Casipe from the HWTC kitchen, and after a few logistics conversations, we ended up with this awesome system: Chef Rossy would send her request for set volumes of produce cut in specific ways to Chef Ricky at the HWTC. For example, she'd ask for five pounds of julienned red peppers or two pounds each of small diced carrots, celery, and onions. Ricky would place the order with 100km Foods, which would deliver the whole ingredients to the HWTC kitchen. The trainees would peel, trim, and chop the vegetables, then pack them up in vacuum-sealed bags. 100km Foods would pick up those processed vegetables and drive them up the street to us. We got our prepped vegetables (at no extra cost), the trainees had the chance to practice their skills for a real customer, and our local supplier made a good sale. They were delivering product to both of our kitchens anyway, and 100km Foods was happy to donate the extra delivery of processed vegetables from HWTC and to Ryerson to make this work. I happened to be in the kitchen one day when 100km Foods arrived with the prepped vegetables from the HWTC. They were beautiful, and I was so happy to know that it was all the produce from our local family farms. Chefs Rossy and Ricky had created a process that worked for both of them, and we were doing it! As I rode the elevator back up to my office, I reminded myself that when you value all of the hands involved in moving food from farm to table, it's a win-win-win situation. There *is* a way to do this, and we were figuring it out.

The real test of our commitment to our values and our in-house production capability came with the PanAm Games in the summer of 2015. Ryerson's athletic centre was the basketball and wheelchair basketball venue, and we were required to provide food services for those events. I was thrilled to be taking this on and to learn about food service in this context. We met with the team who had just come from catering the London Olympics, and I was fascinated to see what the food requirements were like. The two areas of focus were food service (concessions and catering) and waste management, but curiously, there were no actual guidelines about the food served on-site. Of course, the very clear reason for this was that the IOC and the PanAm Games download that responsibility onto the host site, then wash their hands of it. Food is a facilities thing, and in the sports world, food is often little more than an opportunity for corporate sponsorship. This is how we ended up with Olympians lining up for an hour for McDonald's burgers and fries in the Olympic village in Rio and Usain Bolt eating 100 McNuggets a day in Beijing. (Imagine how fast he could have run with real food!)

Here's how it works: the host venue is given a dollar amount per person, for a handful of different groups of people on-site during the games. Athletes, referees, families and VIP, media, security, and volunteers all get different meals, served different ways, at different times. The venues then must figure out how to serve meals that fit within the budget they've been offered. There are a few particular requirements for the athlete meals and for the family and VIP meals, but other than that, venues are free to serve pretty much whatever they want.

When I learned that we were going to be doing this food service, I was determined that even if the meals were very simple, they were all going to be scratch-made, wholesome, and taking full advantage of us being at the peak of the Southern Ontario growing season. This was how we do food at Ryerson, and the PanAm Games were going to be no exception. At the time, our catering chef was David Folkerth, who had come to us from the Real Food for Real Kids kitchen, which prepares and serves thousands of good, wholesome hot lunches to daycare and school kids every day. David shares my values about local sourcing, seasonal eating, and scratch cooking, and he had the added benefit of also really knowing how to pack lots of vegetables and good nourishment into meals for students, on a budget.

I sat down with Chef David and showed him the scope of catering we were talking about, and I asked him honestly if he could pull this off while still maintaining our values around food and hospitality. To this day, I don't know if he really believed he could do it, but he immediately committed to figuring it out. When I heard from the Games organizers that Toronto is the one place in the Americas where there are communities from all of the participating countries — athletes always have someone from their home country cheering them on in the crowd — I realized we should make sure that our menu also included dishes from all of the countries in the Americas, so that familiarity could continue for the athletes, families, volunteers, staff, and spectators. Chef David worked for the better part of a year to build menus for catering to prepare and serve from a big production kitchen that was being built in the athletic centre. We did a tasting for the folks from the PanAm Games a few months out, and they were blown away by the quality, flavour, and variety of our food. We boasted about the fact that we were able to showcase Ontario produce during the Games and that all of our guests would get a good taste of our local harvest. When we told the organizers about our focus on foods of the Americas, they were hugely impressed, and I realized these thoughts had never even crossed their minds. Our ideas worked, but now our task was to figure out how to get the staffing, service, and logistics sorted out to do this for hundreds and sometimes thousands of people a day.

We also had to take our written communications strategy to the next level. The Games had three official languages, English, French, and Spanish, which needed to be on all signage. That sounds simple enough, but when you consider the fact that we wanted to have fresh, seasonal menus with diverse cultural roots with accommodations for vegans, vegetarians, and gluten-free eaters, you will find yourself dizzy with the details and organization required to pull this off. First, Chef David planned and costed out all of the menus. Then Mel got them all translated into French and Spanish and designed a clean and cheerful sign template that told the story of the menu while also still complying with the Accessibility for Ontarians with Disabilities Act (AODA) standards around visual accessibility. Mel and Rory led a training session for the service team on how to use and maintain menu signage. As the venue for the wheelchair basketball competition during the ParaPanAm Games, we had to pay close attention to the positioning of our tables and signage for the large population navigating our spaces in wheelchairs. It was intense and demanding, and I honestly loved watching it all come together. This was like the logistics Olympics, and our team was reaching for the gold.

In the days leading up to the start of the Games, we were full-steam ahead, with food prep already started, a crew still putting the finishing touches on the kitchen, and the technical team from the Games in full move-in mode. Games security restricted access to the loading dock, and the city had put some temporary parking rules out on the street that made it more complicated for our suppliers to navigate. We had to find storage for large orders, since not all of our smaller suppliers were able to make daily deliveries and instead brought a week's worth of food at once.

Here's the thing: we could have easily just decided to serve a menu anchored in the Sysco product listing. Everything would show up at one time, on one skid, wrapped in plastic, and we would be good to go. In fact, most of the other venues took exactly this approach. But we stood by our values, and Chef David, Rory, Tyler, and their teams were ready for the ripples of complication and had created systems and processes that allowed us to serve thousands of fresh, wholesome, delicious meals.

I remember that first day of meal service to the full

suite of guests in the space. The athletes had arrived, media coverage had begun, and baskets were scored. I hung out in the volunteer dining space, watching everything happen. The meals were fresh and colourful, and the service team looked genuinely happy to be there. We had cookies from Andrea for dessert and lovely fresh, local fruit. Vegetarians and vegans were delighted that there were meals for them, and the athletes literally clapped and cheered for the real, wholesome food that they were served during training and competition. One of my best friends is an athletic therapist, and she was working at another venue during the Games. At the end of each day, she'd show me a photo of the food she was served at her venue, and I'd tell her what was on our menu — the meals were worlds apart. Hers were a tour through the Sysco inventory, and I was disappointed that when the stakes got higher, other institutions just rolled over and served thawed, industrial food. For me, it felt crucial that we find a way to scale up our values and make the money work. This was not easy and was often frustrating and bewildering, but we did it! We made change that was scalable and created our own rubric for how to manage diverse, large-scale feeding.

Sadly, and perhaps realistically, not everything during my time at Ryerson was a gold-medal victory, and I learned a lot of hard lessons about meeting students where they are and rolling out change. When I arrived, I learned that the campus was about to become bottled-water free, which was great news, since in Ontario alone, one billion plastic bottles go to landfill every year, where they'll take between 450 and 1,000 years to decompose. Food services had been given a deadline by which we were to stop ordering bottled water and sell out of whatever existing inventory we had. While a move away from bottled water was clearly the way forward environmentally, our revenue was going to take a hit, as we sold just under $20,000 worth of bottled water each month. When the day came, we celebrated that we were all going to be "taking back the tap" instead of consuming (often) imported water from single-use plastic bottles.

What happened almost immediately was an onslaught of people wanting us to fill their reusable water bottles. Our team did whatever they could to help, but some further investigation revealed that the water-filling stations and gooseneck fountain retrofits that were supposed to be installed across campus were not yet in place, which was why people were bombarding us in food services. We set up water canisters in all of our retail spaces and did the very best we could to accommodate these requests.

About a month into this bottled-water ban, Ashlee Collins, our food services GM, shared something really interesting with me. In the first month of the ban, our sales showed the expected dip from the bottled water. But what was unexpected was an increase in sales of bottled pop to almost the exact same dollar figure. When they couldn't get their hands on bottled water, the students bought bottled soda instead. That was entirely the opposite direction we wanted to go in, and I was crushed. But what these sales numbers also told us was that it was less about what was in the bottle and more about the students' love of a resealable, disposable bottled beverage.

I maintain that this was also about habits and the very basic business of changemaking. Not having the filling stations and gooseneck water fountain retrofits ready for the moment the campus eliminated bottled water was a big mistake. When trying to change people's habits, you've got to have something to instantly replace the undesirable habit. You need to make the desired change easy. We should have cut ribbons in front of new filling stations, given reusable bottles to all students, and created some programming to engage students and encourage them to fill their bottles and drink tap water. I'm not saying that this would have prevented the spike in bottled pop sales, but it did offer a major lesson in making change. If I wanted students to stop eating the processed industrial food served all around campus and start eating our scratch-made, locally sourced food, I needed to make sure that the new menu was extensive enough, affordable, and always available. I had to make the new behaviour as easy as the old one.

Another tough lesson came when I focused my attention on snacks and after-hours food options for the campus. We had more than 30 vending machines on campus — about half of them were for bottled beverages and the other half for snacks. The purpose of vending machines is to offer something to eat when the retail operations are not running, which is mostly late at night and sometimes on the weekends. It didn't feel right to me that students would only have the option to eat chocolate bars or bags of chips when our cafés were closed, so I focused on injecting our values into vending. Although I didn't have any control over the Coke contract on campus, I did have some control over those snacks.

I called up Marc Kadonoff from Sweets from the Earth, an organic, vegan bakery making totally delicious sweets that were already packaged and ready for those machines. I also reached out to Peter Neal, one of the two brains behind Neal Brothers, a company that specializes in good snacks. Peter brought me a boxful of delicious things that he thought could work in the vending machines. There were packets of cheesy crackers, gluten-free cookies, fairly traded chocolate bars, real fruit chews, potato chips cooked in good oils, and even little sachets of almond butter that you could squeeze onto an apple, or directly into your mouth for that matter. We did some internal taste testing and started planning the new look for our vending machines.

Obviously, the big question here was whether the students would buy these new snacks. Nothing sells a food product like a taste test, so before we launched these new items, we held an event called Snackfest one Thursday afternoon at prime snacking time. We set up tables and all of our new vendors happily brought samples to share with the campus community. We welcomed students, encouraged them to taste everything, and informed them that they would see these rolled out in all of the campus vending machines in the next week. Students were all very excited about the new snacks, and we had created some fun, buzzworthy programming.

Ultimately, however, my vending experiment was not a success. A couple of months in, we had some tangible numbers to look at, and we saw substantial losses in vending sales. I consulted the food services team member responsible for filling and maintaining the machines, and he told me it was challenging to manage inventory with relatively short expiry dates in 14 machines across campus. Some of our vegan sweets were quite perishable, and he wasn't always able to keep up. He also heard from many students who wanted us to bring back their recognizable brands. They wanted their Kit Kats, M&Ms and Doritos, and they just went elsewhere to get them if the vending machines didn't stock them. While this was disappointing, it also made perfect sense — this was the sort of middle-of-the-road compromise that is often necessary when making change in a place as big as an institution. I brought the corporate branded products back into the machines, but we narrowed that inventory to three of the five display rows in the machines. The remaining two rows offered our values-driven snacks, culled to the bestsellers. Thankfully, vending sales perked back up as a result.

It's a difficult truth, but in the context of the public sector and food service, you can't let your values form a barrier between you and the community you serve. If you rebuild the menu strictly in accordance with values, however sound and legitimate, and nobody buys or eats the food, has this effort worked? Sadly, no, and I was reminded of Janice Sorenson's wisdom about how food is only healthy if it's eaten. I had to learn to be ready to rework and pivot our approach at all times. This wasn't easy, as I felt like I was constantly compromising my vision and values for the sake of generating revenue, but this is an unavoidable reality. The truth is I was trying to untangle eating habits that were a lifetime in the making, and the process is not as simple as swapping in new snacks.

Our campus food overhaul wouldn't be complete without tackling our catering operation that provided meals, snacks, and beverages for the majority of events on campus. Silvana Babikian had been the catering manager with the previous operator, and she was an invaluable resource, bringing experience, passion, connection, and capability. She and I worked together to revise a catering menu that had not been updated or repriced in a very long time. While we did lots of plated and buffet meals, some of our most significant catering business was for platters of fruit, sweets, and cheese, the go-to for meetings, events, and receptions. Every time I would walk through the kitchen, there was someone slicing fruit, portioning squares, and dicing cheese for these platters.

It was a very easy decision to start using Monforte cheese on our catering menu. Monforte Dairy produces beautiful cheeses with local and naturally produced milk from cows, sheep, and goats, and the owner Ruth Klahsen shares our deep commitment to sustainability and embracing change as a path to success. I have known Ruth for years and have been a fan of both her cheese and her attitude towards her business. When she and her team were facing eviction, she started the first cheese CSA and enjoyed extraordinary success.

We had an artisanal cheese platter on our catering menu, and it quickly became the Monforte cheese platter. One day just before convocation, I walked into the catering fridge to chat with Chef David, who was putting away an order. The sturdy metal shelves in that fridge were piled high with wheels of Ruth's cheese. I grabbed David's arm urgently and asked him if we could really afford to buy this much cheese. He smiled at me and said yes, he had costed it all out, and this was a totally affordable purchase. I floated out of the kitchen. I'd see Ruth on Saturday mornings at the market, and she'd give me a hug full of gratitude. I was so glad that we were able to make it work, and the truth is this *should* be the way things are done.

The fruit platter, on the other hand, set off major alarm bells for me. I would see cases of imported berries, melons, grapes, and pineapples arriving in the loading dock week after week, regardless of the season. That fruit was reliably low flavour and usually quite sour.

Those white-cored strawberries didn't actually taste like anything, the melons were just a vehicle for water with a hint of sweetness, and the pineapples actually left a painful, acidic residue in my mouth. For a few months of the year, grapes were little bombs of sweet flavour, but for most of the time, the gutter of your mouth would feel that burny tingle of tannic sourness when you ate them. What's worse is that there would always be leftover fruit on the platters. They would be left out for the service team to help themselves to, but invariably, some fruit would be thrown away. I'd see the fruit in those organics bins in the dish room and shake my head at the long road that so much of that fruit took to get there. "This is the problem," I remember saying directly to that fruity organics bin. "It's a sort of madness that has us importing fruit that doesn't taste good just because we're used to it and it looks pretty." Our obsession with the appearance of a fruit plate has us burning fossil fuels to ship this sad, sour fruit all over the place while we watch the temperature of the planet continue to rise.

In my opinion, a fruit plate in an Ontario winter is a basket of apples. They're whole apples, because slices will brown on a platter, but there may be three different kinds, all from Ontario farms, all totally delicious, and if they don't get eaten, they can be repurposed. In the summer, the platters will drip with Niagara stone fruit and berries from Simcoe county, but in the winter, it's apples. I tasked Chef David to come up with an interesting way to do this so that we didn't have to buy imported fruit. He included dried apples, apple chips, and dried cranberries with the baskets of apples, which I really loved.

From the moment the first fruit platter went out, angry feedback came back. I was very surprised at how passionate people were about this particular issue. People across the campus demanded we return to the "normal" platters. When I told them that our new values around sustainability and local sourcing now excluded those imported fruits, they scolded me and explained "standards" in messages that dripped with condescension. At events, people would meet me and say, "So you're the one who took my fruit platter away," while shaking my hand.

An honest assertion of sustainability is also about putting a stop to certain practices that no longer fit the equation. Those "standards" were likely created before the planet started overheating from the exhaust expelled by the planes, ships, and trucks transporting those Styrofoam-like strawberries and impotent melons all over the planet. I learned very quickly that most people's embrace of sustainability values stops right at the point where they have to start giving up some of their own comfort and convenience. Making hard choices that align with your values is not easy, but the truth was we needed to stop buying that fruit.

I did get one positive message from a colleague, who applauded our decision. She told me that the apple was a perfect snack on the way home and that she loved the change. I was so grateful for some positive feedback that I sent her a basket of apples and a note of thanks.

But the blowback was so curiously intense, I ultimately had to compromise. In winter, a reduced version of the standard-issue imports was available, but the moment enough Ontario fruit was available, we didn't purchase any imports until our local harvest had ended. All I can say is that for a handful of weeks in the summer, those all-Ontario fruit platters were beautiful.

Luckily, we had some hyper local food that could find its way onto campus menus. Ryerson had already made some great investments into growing food on campus, and I walked into an established culture of edible gardens, community volunteers, and market sales of campus produce. As I'm sure you can imagine, for me, this was a gift. Rye's Home Grown was a student club on the Ryerson campus. They had little garden plots all over campus and a devoted crew of students committed to using growing spaces to address some food security issues for the campus community. When I arrived, they were in need of a new administrative home, and food services seemed to be the right fit to take them on.

When I met with the group, they told me about their desire to grow food on the roof of the engineering building. They had already begun exploring this and had gotten clearance from the engineers, but they still needed a home on campus to manage administration and finances, and some organizational support to pull this off. After brainstorming ways to generate revenue, we had a plan! The RHG team would grow food on the quarter-acre space on top of the engineering building. They had a CSA and a table at our weekly farmers' market where they would sell their produce. I agreed that food services would buy whatever was left at a fair price. The income they earned would go back into supplies for planting and harvesting and would pay the small team of staff who managed the operation. One of the most joyful emails I ever wrote as the director of food services was to all of our chefs on campus, telling them that this campus-grown produce would be coming in weekly and that I'd like them to make sure to do something delicious with it and post a sign that communicated the produce's origin to our guests. One of the benefits of opening up your kitchen to scratch cooking is that you can do stuff like this!

We excitedly began planning crops, and the team busily chose seeds and mapped out their season. While we had a full green light from the engineers to grow in about a foot and a half of topsoil, I didn't want to tempt the fates, so I asked the team to prioritize greens and not to grow heavy things like pumpkins, squash, and potatoes. That roof was *not* going to collapse on my watch. The first harvest from the roof was a variety of gorgeous little sprouts. When they brought the bags into the office to show me, I cradled them like they were newborn babies, oohing and aahing at how gorgeous they were.

As the season progressed, we saw the Rye's Home Grown market table get fuller and fuller of their rooftop harvest. I loved seeing the president of the university at the table, picking up green beans and peppers to take home to his family. One afternoon, I saw Mohamed Lachemi, then provost, at the market, and I pressed two cherry tomatoes from the roof, still warm from the sun, into his hand. I smiled and said, "Just put these in your mouth!" He looked at me quizzically but obliged, and I saw the delight spread across his face as the sweetness of that tomato exploded in his mouth. "We grew those on the roof of the engineering building," I told him. His eyes popped open with surprise, and he said, "Now *that's* local!" We laughed, and he thanked me for bringing good food back to campus. I returned to my office, marvelling at the magic of two sun-kissed cherry tomatoes.

At the end of the season, the team triumphantly reported that we had grown two tonnes of organic produce on that quarter-acre rooftop. Taking into account that our harvest was largely leafy greens, that is a serious quantity of food, grown just a few steps from one of the busiest intersections in North America.

Word began to spread about the rooftop growing, and the excitement about what we were doing was palpable. It was quite something to stand there, among rows of kale and chard, and take a full, deep breath that let you get grounded and centered, right in the middle of the city. Volunteers worked joyfully at weeding, tending, and harvesting the produce, and everyone was genuinely happy to be there. Rory Gallagher, one of our catering managers, and I immediately started dreaming about the chicken coop we needed and about where we'd put the jazz trio and cruiser tables for the fundraising receptions that we would hold up there.

Throughout the season, the management team routinely took our front and back of house staff up to the roof to see what was growing. One of my favourite things to see was cooks with their aprons flapping in the breeze, diving in to harvest peppers or tearing off a bit of lemon balm for a taste. Many of our staff were immigrants and had very clear memories of growing food in their home countries. The idea of us growing food on campus made sense to them, and it was lovely to have them tell us the names of the vegetables we were growing in their native languages and to share recipes for things they used to eat as kids. In our second season, Chef Rossy asked the team to grow only yellow chili peppers. Already an undisputed hot sauce making champ, Rossy had the idea of making a rooftop hot sauce and wanted to keep it yellow, with a blue label — true to the RU colours of blue and gold. Those chilies were *hot*, and our sauce was magical and quickly sold out.

One day, Arlene Throness, our lead grower, told me that she had purchased some compost for the farm and that a massive amount of it was going to arrive in a couple of weeks. The challenge before us was to figure out how to get that small mountain of compost up to the roof. I reached out to my friends at Student Affairs to see if they might be interested in helping out and having a fun team-building experience along the way. They were in, and we set the date! On the morning of the move, I arrived at the engineering building to discover that the elevator was down, but we still had to move about 1,200 pounds of compost up six storeys. The incredible Student Affairs team was unphased and with good humour began filling bins that they hauled up the stairs. In just a few hours, we had all of that compost on the roof and spread out onto the beds. Our colleagues from Student Affairs were more than happy to be helpful and do what needed to be done to keep that food growing. To thank this team for their effort, we fed them lunch, and it was wonderful to sit around a table with all of those tired, contented faces.

It quickly became clear to us that something more than just growing food was happening up on that roof. We had volunteer sessions a couple of times a week, and I would visit occasionally. What I always saw were people working cheerfully, hands in the dirt. We would regularly send our staff up to the roof to watch things grow, get a fresh perspective on the campus, and inhale that sweet scent of soil and green things growing. Some of them would return talking about feeling a calm peacefulness among the plants, and student volunteers told us about how they enjoyed getting out of their heads and focusing on their hands in the soil. The mental health benefit of doing something as useful and tactile as weeding and harvesting plants was quite obvious, plus volunteers got to take some of that beautiful food home to enjoy. I was reminded of some advice I received from Mark Freeman, a mental health advocate and innovator. He said, "Health is fuelled by food. No food, no health." While food may be what nourishes you physically, the time spent tending a garden and cooking nurtures you mentally, and our rooftop farm provided a perfect mix of both of those connections for students, staff, and faculty.

Growing some of our own vegetables became a vital part of our campus food culture, and many years later, the rooftop farm is still going strong. They're even training urban farmers and have partnered with different faculties on research projects. They're now selling to local restaurants, which is fantastic news. This team has won awards and continue to be an example for people from other buildings, cities, provinces, and countries who want to learn about how to use urban rooftop space to grow food and animate a community.

I got a wake-up call at a conference in 2014, when Ken Steele, a trend and culture expert for higher education in Canada and the U.S., said a shocking 64 percent of university undergrads were walking around with some form of anxiety. I knew that food services had to do everything we could to make things a little easier for them. During exam season, this anxiety only increased: students were stressed out, profs were swamped with marking, and everyone was a bit worse for the wear. So our retail team starting serving chicken soup more frequently and putting more immune-boosting garlic in the food. And Chef

Rossy made comforting things like mac and cheese and stews that simmered away for hours.

We had a meeting with our frontline service team just before exam season began, and I asked the team for ideas about things they could do to help reduce this stress. A number of staff sweetly suggested that they could offer hugs to students. I loved the instinct but knew there would be some consent issues. Instead, we came up with some encouraging things that the staff could say while handing over a coffee or toasted bagel, like "You'll get through this!" "Hang in there, you'll do just fine!" and "Good luck!" This little shift in understanding our purpose as campus food service changed our frontline staff's sense of what they were doing. Their jobs weren't just about pushing coffee and doughnuts. They were taking good care of students, and that was really something to be proud of.

This conversation got me thinking about how food services could offer some more conscious mental health support to students, staff, and faculty. Mel had been working on some lovely stickers with encouraging messages and helpful tips for surviving exam period. Sometimes what you need is a glass of water or a walk outside, *not* another cup of coffee. We decided to host an event that supported mental health with both something nice to eat and drink and a kind message to soothe hearts and minds. We had received donations of mini scones from Sandra at Baker & Scone and cookies from our supplier, Andrea. The kitchen made a delicious vegan cocoa, and we made a soothing herbal infusion. We put Mel's sweet stickers on the cups of cocoa and tea and held them out with paper bags of scones and cookies for students to grab as they walked by. They didn't even need to stop! We'd say, "Hang in there! Here's a little treat to get through it! Read the sticker on the cup!" And, of course, "That cocoa is vegan!" Our social media feed was a flurry of gratitude and excitement after that little activation. We had made people's days and helped to diffuse stress, and that felt wonderful.

We also made group study snack packs and asked students in the library or student centre to share photos of themselves on social media that illustrated how badly they needed some treats from food services to get them through their studying. We got a lot of awesome photos of students languishing between the stacks. The most pitiful photos won, and Niveen Saleh, our student engagement manager, would figure out where these students were and deliver them a basket of good, yummy study treats. Once the treats were delivered, we'd see a photo of the same group revived and reanimated thanks to their special delivery. This wasn't just about treats, of course, it was about connection. I got teased and scolded for offering free stuff without forcing sales, and while I understood that maintaining and growing sales was vital to our operation, sometimes I like to give something away for free. No strings, no email address, no answer-these-five-questions-first, nothing. Just enjoy this delicious thing.

In one of my early days on the job, I was asked to give a little talk to some of the student leaders in our residences about the changes to food services. I asked Chef David McGann, our residence chef, to make me a simple vegetable minestrone soup to serve at the talk, which he did beautifully. There was half of the tureen leftover, so I wheeled the cart down into the dining room to offer a bowl to students who were studying. Every single one of them was certain that I was some weirdo and that there was a catch. A few students in, I refined my pitch and introduced myself as their new director of food services, before offering them some vegetable minestrone. Every single student accepted a bowl. I could have just wheeled that cart into the dish room and gone home, but I don't like wasting food, and there was an opportunity for connection that I couldn't pass up.

Another campus program that was very close to my heart was the Community Food Room, which was essentially a campus food bank supported by the student union. Like any other food bank, they were not able to fully meet the needs of the community. If there are students who are unable to afford to feed themselves, the administration needs to be involved and paying attention; this responsibility should not be left to the student union. On behalf of the administration, I reached out to see how food services could help. We offered access to suppliers for wholesale pricing and produce seconds to make their purchasing dollars go as far as possible and set up a system for sharing leftover food with the Community Food

Room at the end of the day or after particular events. Wasting food is a bad idea in general, but it's almost cruel to do this when we know that there are hungry students on campus. When food services supports academic excellence, it concerns itself with issues like student hunger, food access, and the affordability of its meals.

At this time in my life, I was struggling with the idea of whether or not to have children of my own. As a single person, I was leaning towards the idea of not having any, for fear of not being able to handle it all by myself. So many times on my drive home after events like move-in day or the launch of a new menu, my heart would be beaming from having such a great interaction with students, and I would feel the swell of real gratitude. I realized that while I might not have a child of my own, I have the opportunity to take really good care of hundreds, if not thousands, of other people's children . . . and maybe that was even better.

Ryerson was my longest institutional project — two and a half years — and with that amount of time we were really able to start growing a culture of good food on campus. Word spread to other campuses too, and the senior Chartwells folks told me that they were getting lots of requests from other accounts for the Ryerson package. They would smile and say, "As long as you have a Joshna, we can give you the Ryerson." Ryerson had leadership and vision, and Chartwells brought logistics and capacity to the table, and together, we were able to build and deliver delicious, inclusive, and sustainable food service to the campus. I would get calls on a pretty regular basis from other campuses who were at various stages of negotiation with their own food service contract, with pretty specific questions about how we navigated certain bits of the process. I was always happy to answer those questions and even did some consulting for a couple of universities.

Some of the most substantial information sharing happened through Meal Exchange, a student network across Canada working to build more sustainable, nourishing, and student-driven campus food systems. A couple of summers before I started my job at Ryerson, I was asked to be a resource for the Meal Exchange team, who were looking to build a National Student Food Charter. This was an exciting and pioneering effort, and at the end of it, we were left with a document that clearly outlined what students wanted from their campus food and the kind of role they felt food should play in students' lives. I brought this charter to the table when we were creating our vision and RFP at Ryerson. If we already have a clear notion of what students want, let's use that language in how we build campus food service and how we engage third-party operators. I actually cut and pasted portions of the charter right into the RFP, and this was another beautiful example of how making change is easier with an existing set of values. If students have taken the time to articulate their vision, the least we should do is listen.

My colleagues on campuses across the country are hearing more and more from students about the need for wholesome, sustainably sourced food on campus and transparent contracts that involve students in the process. There are a few universities that already uphold these values and have been leading the way for many years before I showed up on the scene. At the University of Guelph, the values around locally sourced, sustainably produced food have been alive on this agricultural campus for many years. Mark Kenny, the university's procurement manager, has been instrumental in building U of G's culture of good food. When I started working at Ryerson, I joined Mark at a Mennonite produce auction and was in awe that he was purchasing such gorgeous local produce for a university campus. There were skids of plump, juicy strawberries; cases of fresh eggs; big bags of heirloom carrots; and an incredibly talented auctioneer moving from lot to lot, managing bids and making sales. Mark had figured out a system that works, and the kitchen was ready to handle whole produce like this. Later on, during a tour of U of G's kitchen, I all but chained myself to the counter in the incredible processing room that they had built to allow their kitchen team to take maximum advantage of the local harvest by processing and preserving fruits and vegetables for use during the winter months. Throughout my time at Ryerson, I was running to keep up with Mark, and I've learned a lot about how effective the purchaser can be in influencing the kind of food served in an institution. Since then, Mark has become a friend and trusted ally, and I recently heard that U of G has been consistently at 40 percent local food procurement, with a boost to 55 percent during the growing season. What is very clear is that the writing is on the wall about the need for better, more nourishing, accessible, and sustainable campus food, and there are ripples of action happening across Canada.

And in the U.S., 72 campuses have signed on to the Healthier College Initiative from the Partnership for Healthy America (PHA), which requires schools to adhere to commitments that include a minimum number of fruits, vegetables, and whole grains available at each meal; plant-based options; better labelling; free water; and health and wellness programming. Since these initiatives often come at an extra expense that may be harder for minority-serving institutions to take on, the PHA helps find donors who can address some of the food-based racism that afflicts these communities.

Real change anywhere happens *very* slowly. In a bureaucracy, it's sloth-like. I remember repeatedly feeling so defeated by how long it took to get things done, but I always played along and filled out the necessary forms. It's this messy, unsexy underbelly stuff that really determines the lasting impact of change. And this slow and steady progress didn't seem so sloth-like to others: around my departure from Ryerson, one of my colleagues said,

"The really amazing thing was how quickly you managed to make so much change happen! Things never happen that fast in this place."

I left my position at Ryerson in December 2015, when a change of leadership meant my values no longer had the administrative support they needed. Over the course of a few months, it became very clear to me that the future of the program I had built was now out of my hands. Turning away from my baby was perhaps one of the most difficult things I've ever done. Since then, Ryerson appears to have distanced themselves from rebuilding campus food. The team that I worked with was gradually dismantled, and different priorities were pursued. What's more disappointing is that the leadership that made these detrimental blows to our food program has since moved on from Ryerson. I can't help but lament that the people who have really lost out are the students, the very population of people we were supposed to be serving.

Curiously, I was recently invited by the business school at Ryerson to give a talk about building values-based initiatives. It was the first time I had returned to that campus since leaving it four years ago. Students and faculty talked a lot about their dissatisfaction with current food services, and I discovered there's a campus group called Ryerson Students for Food Security making the same complaints and advocating for the same improvements as their predecessors in 2013. I was sad to hear that they were back in the same place they were six years ago, but I offered encouragement and, I'll confess, also stoked the fire with a reminder that it was student outrage that brought me onto that campus to make change and likely only student outrage could make any change happen again.

I am as convinced as ever that rebuilding the culture of food in our schools is worth our attention and effort, but this process has taught me how much this all rests on having the right person with the right values in power as your champion, along with some guaranteed time to make and implement change. Sustainability and a culture of good food need to be a formal part of an institution's core values, otherwise an entire culture is vulnerable to and dependent on people who can come and go. I know now that any projects I do in the future will require an institution to make a longer, deeper commitment. It's going to take at least three to five years for us to untangle and rebuild decades of industrial food. A restaurant uses an arc of five years to determine its viability, and the money often doesn't make any sense until well after the third year. This change is necessary, it's possible, and it's viable, but it won't happen overnight, and we have to come at it with fair expectations and real commitment to doing it properly.

Before my departure, I did some exit interviews with students, staff, and faculty who were close to food services. They understood what we were trying to do, and they were proud to be a part of an institution that was a leader in change. But perhaps the most significant response came from a student who said that the new menu, signage, and communication told them that the administration were genuinely invested in their well-being. I'd become the caretaker of the students' revolution, and I couldn't have been happier that they gave me a passing grade.

CHAPTER 5

SOCIAL GASTRONOMY
Giving Food a Seat at the Table

"The best way to find yourself is to lose yourself in the service of others."
—— MAHATMA GANDHI

I didn't fall in love with cooking at my mother's side or at the stainless steel counters of a culinary school, but at an ashram in the foothills of the Himalayan mountains. I wasn't there to learn to cook, either: I was a religious studies graduate with plans to go for walks, eat mangoes, and grapple with my own existential dilemma. But cooking found me. Or rather the aunties who worked in the ashram kitchen found me, and they were particularly concerned about the fact that I didn't know how to cook, because *how* was I going to find a husband?! I knew enough to get me through university and could do some pretty delicious things with a can of chickpeas, some pasta, and cream cheese . . . but I didn't know anything about cooking Indian food. At the same time, I'm the oldest female child in an Indian family, so there was really no way I was escaping work in the kitchen. For my whole childhood, I watched my mom and my aunties tip roasted ground spices into pans with a sort of alchemic confidence. I would clean vegetables, chop onions, wash rice, and do the dishes while listening to the sound of spices sputtering in hot oil, the chatter of the women working around me, and the distinct sound of their bangles hitting the sides of the pots they stirred.

I was 24 at the time, and the clock was ticking on my expiry date as a desirable bride, so one day the aunties dragged me away from my angst-filled notebook and into the kitchen to save me before it was too late. That afternoon, I made the dough for, portioned, rolled, and toasted about 60 chapatis, with the coaching of two aunties who watched me like they were my prospective mothers-in-law.

I went back the next day, and the day after that, and soon enough I had a daily kitchen shift. In the Hindu context of the ashram, a kitchen is a sacred space, and that means you work barefoot, leaving your shoes (and also your shit) at the door. I chopped vegetables in my lap on the floor, stirred big pots of food over a single propane burner, and rolled chapati dough for hundreds on my haunches, and I loved every moment of it. It turns out the solution to my existential crisis wasn't in the foothills but in the kitchen. The small kitchen crew and I became great friends, and my two aunties were happy, and I'm sure relieved, that they had intercepted my tragic spiral into spinsterhood.

I learned a lot about cooking in the Indian kitchen during that time, but perhaps the most profound lesson was about the power and influence of a cook. One day the head cook was in a bad mood. He was short with all of us and banged things around in the kitchen while he worked. We worked mostly in tense silence. When we served that food, I was amazed to see a wave of crankiness and indigestion wash over the whole dining hall full of mostly monks and nuns, who were thoughtfully engaged in managing their own emotional states and were not immune to the dark cloud that we were serving in those pots of dal and rice. Thankfully, this also worked the other way. There was one day when the head cook had been visited by his girlfriend, leaving him with a sparkle in his eye and a spring in his step. His cheery mood was infectious; we played music in the kitchen and laughed and joked around while we prepared lunch. When we served those pots of food, I watched closely as everyone took in a portion of that good mood on their plates. People who arrived a bit quiet and scowling left the dining hall smiling, and some even stopped to thank us and share a little joke. I learned cooks have both an incredible responsibility and opportunity to have an exponential impact on people with their food.

Even if you don't buy into my *Like Water for Chocolate* philosophy, it's undeniable that good food, and the attitude and effort that creates it, can change people's lives. I first heard the term "social gastronomy" from the Basque Culinary Centre in Spain, which had created an award to recognize chefs around the world using food to create social change. Social gastronomy is the work of chefs who step into the role of activists and advocates for food and for communities. We use our power and influence to make choices about procurement, kitchen management, labour, menu creation, and service that promote justice, equity, and inclusion. As chefs, I believe that we should be concerned about how people are eating all of the time, not just when they're at our tables. We can use our kitchens as platforms to advocate for the kind of change we want to see in our food system. Social gastronomy also redefines what it means to be a chef in a way that is more inclusive and dynamic. Chefs work in kitchens, wherever they may be — food trucks, farmers' markets, quick serve restaurants, hospitals, schools, drop-in centres, and prisons — to serve both the food and the people. Social gastronomy makes space for the kind of chef that I am and the values that I have about food.

I started this book with a conversation about hospitality and sustainability as guiding principles, and in all of the social gastronomy conversations I've had, these concepts are always the foundation. Social gastronomy is about using the values of the kitchen and dining room to animate other food spaces in a way that promotes justice, ecological stewardship of the land, and thriving communities. If sustainability and hospitality are not present, it's not social gastronomy.

Fortunately, chefs are well equipped to be activists. We often work with less-than-ideal circumstances. We have to be innovators and troubleshooters, often simultaneously. We figure it out, we make it happen, and regardless of what's going on in the kitchen, we get those plates out on time. We can make sustainability, equity, and hospitality the foundation of the way people eat everywhere. This is more than just an opportunity: this is a responsibility.

Social gastronomy takes many different forms: sometimes that means cooking delicious food in the middle of a muddy farmer's field in the windy rain, as it did for about 100 chefs in September 2011. Deceptive developers and miners had been buying parcels of land in Melancthon county north of Toronto, claiming they were planning to grow potatoes. When they filed paperwork that revealed they'd build a 900-plus hectare megaquarry in the prime farmland instead, the community fought back with Foodstock, a fundraiser and protest on some of the land that had not been sold to these developers. The event was spearheaded by the Canadian Chefs' Congress and its president, Chef Michael Stadtländer, who lives and works in the region and thought we should push back against this proposed destruction of our local food system by occupying the land and resisting with our cooking. Nearby farmers and producers donated food, and chefs from across the country signed up to cook tantalizing mouthfuls to feed guests.

Local chefs opened up their kitchens to chefs from out of town, and there was palpable excitement. As a cook, I really appreciated the opportunity to actually do something to support this cause, and I know I wasn't alone. This was a chance for us to walk our talk, and our whole food community was in on it. It was not hard to find volunteers, and people generously helped to arrange rides, share equipment and fridge space, and do whatever else was necessary to get this food cooked and served out there in the woods. I had my own booth and wanted to make something simple and delicious. There was lots of kale available, as well as cornmeal and dairy, and I decided to offer the buttery cornbread that I had made regularly for lunch at The Stop, topped with kale and onions that we would sauté over a fire on-site with ber-bere, a chili-heavy African spice blend. I was really into the idea of the smokiness from the fire mixing with the heat of the chilies in that kale. I remember being in the kitchen the night before, baking cornbread and chopping kale. There is something about that moment, the night before a big event like this — when all of us were busy cooking for the same meal and cause — that is magical. As your own dish comes together, you can feel the event and all those good intentions coming together too — a kind of delicious convergence.

Organizers guessed 15,000 to 20,000 people would attend, and chefs were asked to make as many por-tions as they were able to. It had rained for a couple of days beforehand, and the ground was wet and muddy. Cheerful volunteers with ATVs drove us all to our sta-tions in the forest, and thankfully, it stopped raining just as the event began. The day was blustery, and it was hard to keep our fires lit. We were still sautéing some of the kale when the first wave of guests started to arrive. Over the course of the day, 28,000 people flowed through the misty fields and forest. There was a constant lineup of at least 20 people at my station, and we had to drastically reduce the size of our portions, just to give a little something to everyone. Music from the nearby stage drifted through the trees, as crowds gathered to watch treasured artists like Sarah Harmer and Jim Cuddy play a few songs in the drizzle. Chefs who had run out of food came over to help those of us who still had a supply, and even though we were freezing, and the metal tongs we served with kept slipping out of our gloved hands, the energy was high, and everyone was thrilled to be there. All told, we raised a whopping $107,000 from that mammoth crowd and got 130,000 people to sign an online petition to stop the quarry. It was an incredible show of solidarity from the community and a tremendously successful effort by chefs to protest and protect our farmland. Ultimately, the developers pulled out and the deal dissolved. This was a big win for the community and a brilliant example of what can happen when the entire food community unites to defend its values.

The social gastronomy movement is not without its heroes, and British chef Jamie Oliver is definitely one of these. Over the course of his more than 20 year career, he has made the kitchen exciting and approachable with his vast collection of television shows and cookbooks. While Oliver is often credited with getting more people (particularly men) making delicious food and for waging a revolution on school lunches, I have a slightly different appreciation for him. To me, he is a great example of a chef who understood the power and opportunity of his platform as a celebrity and used it to talk about social issues and make change. I respect and admire that. Jamie Oliver was also the first chef I had heard of who was referred to as a chef/activist, and I loved it instantly. He's the one who showed me the kind of impact that chefs could have outside of their restaurants, and he has inspired me to find my own way to do this.

Chef Daniel Giusti also felt the call to reform school food. He left his position as head chef at globally celebrated Noma in Copenhagen to create Brigaid, an organization that works to put scratch-made, wholesome food into American public schools. In their first three years, they served over two million healthy, affordable school lunches. I met Dan at a social gastronomy summit in Miami, and we instantly clicked and spent a few hours talking about our work. To meet another chef trying to untangle an institutional food system was a gift! He shared my deep commitment to honest, simple food and believed that there had to be a way to make it work for kids in schools. Chef Dan and I have gone through a lot of the same challenges and triumphs as we've tried to improve school food, and I am so grateful to have an ally with such strong shared experience. Here's the way he describes Brigaid's first two years, in a post on his social media feed: "We haven't made any money, we haven't been able to collect sufficient data that concretely proves what we are doing is important. [But] in the end, there is no question our work is so important, in fact essential . . . we feed kids. Let's do this, my friends."

Over in Italy, Chef Massimo Bottura's Osteria Francescana in Modena has held the position of first or second best restaurant in the world for the past five years. Chef Massimo has leveraged his restaurant's "world's best" position to draw attention to an issue that he feels passionately about: hunger and food waste. Starting first in Milan during the Food Expo in 2015, Chef Massimo and his wife, Lara Gilmore, created Refettorio Ambrosiano, a cafeteria that uses surplus food to feed homeless and street-level people. Massimo and his team created a network to collect and deliver surplus food that would have otherwise been thrown away and brought in a parade of some of the world's best chefs to cook lunches in this special kitchen. The food was simple but thoughtfully prepared with whatever ingredients were available. People were served at the table with dignity and hospitality, as though they were in any one of those chefs' home restaurants. Even after the expo, the Refettorio remained, there are now Refettorios in Milan, Rio de Janeiro, London, and Paris. I was honoured to be invited to cook a meal at the Refettorio Gastromotiva in Rio during the Olympic Games in 2016, and on a recent trip to the U.K., I joined the team at the Refettorio Felix in London one morning to cook lunch. Both of these visits reminded me so much of lunch service at The Stop, and I learned that it doesn't matter where in the world you are, for a chef, feeding really hungry people is good for the soul.

Social gastronomy is also well suited to disaster relief, because food and the sustenance and comfort it brings is something people will always need. After Hurricane Maria tore up Puerto Rico in September 2017, government aid was slow to arrive, when it did at all, and hundreds of thousands of people were living without access to food and water. Chef José Andrés, a celebrated chef with restaurants across the U.S., including a training centre for aspiring chefs, founded World Central Kitchen, an organization that responds to the need for food on the ground during a disaster. With this network, he used on-the-ground connections and his own money to get teams of cooks into local kitchens across the island, including one in a sports arena, where they were able to cook meals for the masses. Chefs and suppliers from across the continent sent food and service supplies over to Puerto Rico, and Chef José and the WCK team were able to take swifter, more effective action than the Red Cross, Salvation Army, or FEMA, which did not have any of those local connections. In total, they served more than 2 million meals and proved that chefs are another kind of vital first responder. The *New York Times* described this scenario beautifully, by saying that "with an ability to network quickly, organize kitchens in difficult circumstances, and marshal raw ingredients and equipment, chef-led groups are creating a model for a more agile, local response to catastrophes." In his book entitled *We Fed an Island: The True Story of Rebuilding Puerto Rico, One Meal at a Time*, Chef José writes, "Chefs understand how to create order out of chaos, just as they know how to control the fire to cook great meals. There were lots of moments when we didn't know what to do in the early days. The conversation would go like this: *What the fuck do we do next? Okay, let's keep cooking. That's a good plan!* Reading that, I laughed out loud — those moments are all too familiar.

Sometimes, social gastronomy isn't about who is at the table but who is in the kitchen. In Toronto, Chef Suzanne Barr created a beloved restaurant called Saturday Dinette, serving some of the most delicious plates of food anywhere in the city. One of the foundational pillars of the Dinette was offering opportunities to women of colour to train and work both front and back of house positions in the restaurant as a pathway into the industry. I have always marvelled about how women are the ones cooking the bulk of the world's food, but men have figured out how to get paid to do it. Historically, professional kitchens have been notoriously exploitative environments, and this culture often romanticizes gruelling labour, poor treatment, low wages, and violence — all of which tend to be worse for women and people of colour. Kitchens that don't protect the human rights of all of their employees are fundamentally unsustainable. Chef Suzanne's kitchen not only avoided toxic masculinity, but her thoughtful use of her kitchen has opened up access to careers and employment for a whole community of people while also broadening our ideas about who chefs are.

Even if food isn't the main focus, it can still be a kind

of magical tool. People of all stripes will always enjoy receiving a delicious, well-made thing to eat, and it can be a great way to support other efforts. It'll fuel protestors and community forums, and it'll draw people to your information booth and nourish busy organizers. As Julia Turshen writes in her book *Feed the Revolution*, "Resistance, just like any other active thing, needs to be fed in order to sustain." And if you need to get something done, there is no better lure or wheel-greaser than a tasty plate of food. It was a given that all of The Stop's programming would include meals or snacks, because everyone would rather be at a meeting or event that included food. Garden volunteers went home with a bag of local, organic produce, and my kids after-school program was all about making delicious snacks that were devoured shortly after they were cooked. In my work in hospitals, I would take something we were experimenting with in the kitchen up to the VP's office, and a little bowl of fresh strawberries helped a lot when I was trying to get the folks in accounts payable to allow me to purchase from non-approved suppliers. On a university campus, all of the prizes for our contests were good-food experiences, and students were frequently enticed into conversation using yummy freebie treats. I would always take some produce from the roof or the farmers' market up to the executive offices. I can make all kinds of compelling arguments to executives about the value of investing in growing food on campus, but a carrot pulled out of the dirt on the roof of the engineering building and still warm from the sun is sometimes much more powerful.

To my fellow chefs, have you ever felt that the restaurant life wasn't for you, or that there are issues in the world that you want to address, but you still want to cook? Try something different. Re-evaluate your purchasing and the carbon footprint of your kitchen. Maybe it means that you go to work in a community food space, or you use your restaurant to model a more just labour culture, or you create a connection with a local food organization to supply soups for their community meals. Or maybe you make a few extra sandwiches every week to share with hungry folks in your neighbourhood. There are countless meaningful roles for us to play as advocates and change agents, in addition to being cooks. Your communities need you! With social gastronomy, a kitchen isn't just cooking up mouth-watering meals: it's a venue for conversation, resistance, and revolution.

CONCLUSION

"Another world is not only possible, she is on her way.
On a quiet day, I can hear her breathing."
—— ARUNDHATI ROY, AUTHOR AND ACTIVIST

In the fall of 2017, I was invited to Berlin to do a talk about my work in institutions. My host was Studio Olafur Eliasson, a wonderfully creative and engaged community of around 90 craftspeople, artists, technicians, administrators, archivists, and others anchored in the work of the artist Olafur Eliasson. The studio is exactly what you would expect from a busy, creative workshop, with one main difference: there's also a full kitchen, with a team of cooks — artists in their own right — led by Victoria, Olafur's sister. Four days a week, Victoria and her team cook and serve an organic vegetarian lunch to the entire team. That's right, four out of five workdays, the entire studio team stops working and takes a seat in a big dining room where they connect with colleagues and enjoy food. In this modern world, everyone stopping to sit down to eat a meal is nothing short of radical political action. The kitchen has a relationship with a nearby organic farm, and their menu is guided by the harvest. The studio was going to host an event for the public where I would speak about my work, and we'd have a discussion about the challenges of rebuilding institutional food.

Victoria also invited me to join them in the kitchen during the day to cook lunch for the team, which I was so delighted to do. They were keen on me making some Indian food, so we had a simple fall lunch of chana masala, butternut squash curry, fresh carrot salad, and cumin yogurt, all using the local harvest. We had a lovely time together in the kitchen; I felt an instant kindred connection with Victoria's food philosophy and her willingness to do things differently.

Besides lunch, there is a full coffee bar and fridges with organic juices, sparkling water, and a few bits of chocolate that were readily available for a nominal cost (if any at all). All of the lunch leftovers are placed in a designated spot, and everyone is given a glass jar, which they are encouraged to use to take home those leftovers. My head was spinning with how dreamy and thoughtful this all was — I was witnessing organizational values being put into action. I was seeing the thoughtful creation of a food culture that was guided by nourishing mind and body, ecological stewardship of the land, and human connection, and the incredibly vibrant, creative, engaged, and thriving community of people who are undoubtedly a product of that food culture.

Victoria gifted me a copy of the book that the kitchen at

SOE had published, and I noticed the foreword was written by Alice Waters. I smiled, shook my head, and yelled, "Of course!" Of course, Alice was dear friends with Olaf, and, of course, she was connected to something as innovative and thoughtful as this studio's food program. These folks really understood that there is a place for chefs in a community of artists and that the dining table is a perfect venue for a political and artistic discussion.

You may think an Icelandic artist's studio is a long way from a public hospital, but The Stop's values create a similar culture. And if we can foster that environment in a community food organization, why not a hospital? While I understand and embrace the need for a financial argument, I really resist the idea that feeding people proper, healthy food needs to make good business sense or serve a bottom line. Investing in the improvement of food in public institutions is important because it's the right thing to do, full stop. What we need to remember is that the current "affordable" model for institutional food service is not working, and we have all just accepted the reality of this woefully inadequate offering and adapted our behaviour to work around it. We are failing our most vulnerable while also wasting money, food, and contributing to the climate crisis.

We have to spend money, so let's spend it more wisely. Money spent with the exclusive purpose of keeping costs as low as possible will yield a very low return on investment. But the extra $0.33 a person we spent on that turkey dinner supported local farmers and businesses, nourished patients, avoided waste, increased staff morale, and brought joy to people who were having a tough time. I've witnessed first-hand how a commitment to local sourcing, by even just one institution, can nurture and strengthen our local agricultural economy and local small businesses. "The ultimate goal is that people be able to eat goodness," said Rosalinda Guillén, a farmworker justice leader in Washington State. "Your plate of food in front of you is a reflection of what's going on in your community."

An institution that's leading the charge on mitigating climate change can (and should) use its operation, spending, and influence to support regenerative, sustainable, organic agriculture. Currently, institutional spending is dominated by corporations, and money virtually always goes to a head office somewhere outside of the community. Here's what this looks like on the ground. Remember, for every dollar spent initially in the farm sector, a total of $2.24 travels through the economy. Shouldn't public funds be spent in a way that actually advances an institution's values? Ordering from massive corporate distribution catalogues may be the cheapest option, but *all* of the money leaves our community. Shouldn't purchasing that has a domino impact on the local economy be the more responsible, transparent, and effective way to spend public money? The way that actually results in the largest public good? I am reminded once again of the wisdom of strawberry farmer Morris Gervais, who noted that we were "using Ontario money to buy Ontario food to feed Ontario patients."

And finally, we know that 45 percent of hospital patients are malnourished when they arrive at the hospital. In many cases, this malnourishment has exacerbated whatever ailment has brought them to the hospital in the first place. If we serve patients real, good food, they're more likely to eat it. If patients eat, they're able to heal and rebuild their strength, and the sooner they do that, the sooner they can be discharged and sent home. Ultimately, this is an argument in favour of a preventative approach to health care. Similarly, if students eat wholesome, delicious food, it feeds their bodies *and* their brains, opening up their attention spans and facilitating learning. And based on my knowledge and experience, a good, thoughtful plate of food will restore a prisoner's dignity and humanity, which is a much more effective starting point for rehabilitation. Institutions are places where we learn, heal, and grow. And for such important work, we need proper fuel.

During my time at The Stop, our mission was to build more community food security. FoodARC, a Canadian food research organization, describes community food security as a state "when all community residents have access to enough healthy, safe food through a sustainable food system that maximizes community self-reliance and social justice." We called our work community food animation — the package of programs and initiatives that build and nurture community food security. Food banks, dining programs, urban agriculture, breakfast programs in schools, children's cooking programs, and farmers' markets are just some examples of community food animation. While the context is different, all of the work I've done in public institutions to rebuild food service and food culture is also community food animation. When you really look at it, our institutions are food-insecure communities. Patients, long-term care residents, students, prisoners, teachers, doctors, nurses, support staff, and administrators do not have access to enough healthy, good food.

Where food security and a robust food culture are absent, you can use community food programs to bring these spaces back to life. We know that with food, holistic approaches work best, as food is linked to so many aspects of our daily lives, in personal and communal ways. On the ground in a hospital, this is about wholesome, scratch-made food on patient meal trays. It's about menus that are diverse and that support healing and wellness. But it's also about communication from farms and kitchens with encouraging messages as patients get better. It's about a policy that protects mealtimes and uses volunteers to support patients to get food into their mouths with kindness and dignity. And it's about opportunities for the whole hospital community to learn more about wholesome eating, sustainable farming, and simple ways to cook themselves some good food.

On a post-secondary campus, the first move is always to put food on the plates that is wholesome, delicious, and good value for money spent. But it also requires having a transparent process for awarding food service contracts and a set of values that guide the way food is purchased, prepared, and served on the campus. It's about communication and signage that explains why certain vendors were chosen, what happened to the bottled water, or why the price of a grass-fed burger is $0.25 higher. And it's about cooking classes for students and opportunities to grow food on campus. Food culture is about how food lives in a community, and food security is about access to that food culture. A thriving culture is the desired state, and security opens the door to the party.

I believe much of the responsibility for any change to institutional food services lies directly at the feet of government. In this province, and many others, government budget cuts are largely responsible for the rapid deterioration of institutional meals. In a country where health care, education, and the prison system are all publicly funded institutions, this is largely the government's mess to clean up. The good news is they can also have an enormous impact — by offering earmarked funds to improve and sustain food services and by creating public policy that connects the public sector to local agriculture, small business, and the local economy. As Lori Stahlbrand, executive director of the Toronto Food Policy Council, says, "Good food policy automatically and inherently means good agriculture, health, environment, economic, and education policy."

Another opportunity lies in investing in supporting institutions to make the transition back to scratch cooking. The grim reality is that no institution can afford the cost of reinstalling exhaust hoods, training staff on a new menu, or even experimenting with some new menu ideas, and this is precisely what stands in the way of any real change. A government granting stream that covered the cost of retrofitting a kitchen and some development and training for the kitchen team would make it much easier for institutions to make the change to produce wholesome, scratch-made meals. In both of the hospital projects I worked on and at Ryerson, we received grant money from the provincial government, via the Greenbelt Fund. The incredible learning and building that we did as a result of that funding has been crucial to making change and to providing me with the knowledge and experience I have to put onto these very pages to share. What's more, there were many other projects around the province similar to ours, and all of them got their start with some of that Greenbelt money. Unfortunately, that funding dried up quickly, and with it went lots of amazing projects that were changing the game and gaining some solid momentum. Without real investment, there can be no real change.

That said, there are people all across the country who have been working for decades to try to meet increasing community needs and rebuild our food system. We're doing it the hard way, because of a pretty solid lack of engagement from government about these issues. So, a government first needs to invest in research and learning: travel around the country, talk to people, learn what communities have already built, how it's working, and what they still need. People on the ground have been doing this without government involvement for many years, and that needs to be acknowledged and respected.

Governments can also help articulate some core values, and they can support and protect those values with comprehensive, viable public policy. That's when the change can get exponential. Take the city of Boston, for example, which recently adopted a Good Food Purchasing Policy (GFPP), which offers "a framework for buying local, sustainable, and humanely sourced food." After two years of purchasing with this policy, the city was able to boost the percentage of local produce used in city-run facilities from 9 to 75 percent. According to the GFPP, this has meant $12 million in its supply chain to purchase local produce. Alexa Delwiche, the executive director for the Centre for Good Food Purchasing, which developed the GFPP, explains it like this: "I think the really powerful piece to this is that once a public institution has adopted a policy, that policy really becomes one [that belongs to] both the institution and the community. It's an opportunity for the community to continue engaging public officials and the public institution and hold them accountable to the values they've adopted." More freshly prepared local food in institutions, a values-based purchasing policy, substantial investment in local agriculture, a process that is transparent and accountable: this, my friends, sounds like a much better way to use public money. Government can really help those of us on the ground across the country with public policy like the GFPP that asserts wholesome food as a vital priority for *all* of us. I will happily engage with any political party offering a sincere effort to restore and invest in community food security, because food has to be a non-partisan issue. All of our party leaders need to be much more concerned about national food insecurity and the real vulnerabilities of our food system. Let's face it, the truth is that the government is also a public institution that is sorely in need of a new food culture.

By now, I hope you're all charged up and ready to do something. The good news is there's lots that can be done right at the grassroots level. Communicating with local representatives and elected officials is a great start. It identifies you as a concerned member of the community, and it establishes a connection, should any possibilities take root. But after the emails are sent, there is also an opportunity for some more active communications. Government meetings are (mostly) open to the public, and many offer citizens the opportunity to give a deputation about an issue of concern. Take some miserable institutional food into a city council or even a parent-teacher association meeting and use the food as a tool to get a conversation started. If you find yourself in the hospital, use your voice as a patient to let the administration know that the food service isn't good enough and needs to be taken more seriously. Remember that patient satisfaction matters. And consider some of your own habits and how you can use your purchasing dollars to vote for a more sustainable food system. Making a commitment to buying locally grown, organic food, even just some of the time, is a great way to start. Think about your own relationship with food and the degree to which it does (or doesn't) nurture your good health. Maybe it'll be more inspiring to make lunches for your kids when you think about packing some life force into those meals. What's happening with institutional food is part of our bigger, societal disconnection from our food, and the action for change needs to be diverse, committed, and doable.

We must remember that these are *our* institutions: we built them, and if they're no longer serving us well, it's our job to change them. Change is challenging, but it *is* possible — we just have to remember to choose it. So many people are inherently resistant to change or disrupting the status quo, but I cannot watch an outdated system continue to degrade both the people and the planet. We have to embrace some new ideas, and we need to be fearless about it. So many people I talk to expect that I would have come up with a new risk-free model for institutional food service. But the truth is the only sure thing is that what brought us to this point in our history is not what is going to take us into the future. Innovation and fresh ideas are crucial for our success and survival. Our increasingly corporate institutions don't like risk, but doing nothing is risky too. It lays our people, our planet, and our future generations firmly on the line.

Food is our common denominator as humans. We need it to heal, to grow, and to thrive. It's a source of strength, joy, connection, and life. Good food nourishes us, and it's time for us do the same for our food system. So let's take back dignity, hospitality, sustainability, and equality. And let's use our resources in a way that reflects these values. Let's take back community kitchens, hospital trays, student cafeterias, and prison mess halls. Let's reinvest in the land and the people who work it. Let's nourish the people we love and the people we've never met. Let's put human connection back into our food and at the centre of our food system, and let's allow it to guide us back to health, wellness, and each other. And let's never, ever gum through a sad, stodgy egg-salad sandwich again.

RECIPES

CARROT PINEAPPLE MUFFINS

MAKES 12

These are the muffins that Debbie Lennox and I worked so hard to perfect. They're wholesome, delicious, easy to make, and perhaps the perfect thing to take to someone in the hospital!

INGREDIENTS

¾ cup all-purpose flour
¾ cup whole wheat flour
1 cup granulated sugar
1 tsp baking soda
1 tsp baking powder
1 tsp salt
1 tsp cinnamon

⅔ cup vegetable oil

2 eggs

1 cup carrot, grated

½ cup crushed pineapple

1 tsp vanilla

METHOD

1. Preheat oven to 350°F. Grease a muffin pan or line it with paper liners and set aside.

2. Combine flours, sugar, baking powder, baking soda, salt, and cinnamon in a mixing bowl and set aside.

3. In another bowl, combine oil, eggs, carrot, pineapple, and vanilla. Add wet ingredients to dry ingredients and combine until mixture comes together and all the flour has been incorporated.

4. Bake for 25 minutes, or until a tester inserted into a muffin in the centre of the pan comes out clean.

5. Taste one, then write to your local government about how good these would be for hospital patients.

WHOLEGRAIN TEA BISCUITS

MAKES 12

These biscuits give you the nutritional benefit of whole grains while also offering flaky, buttery layers. I will never forget how good it felt to serve these to the mother-and-baby unit on a cold February morning.

INGREDIENTS

2 cups spelt or red fife flour
    (or 1 cup wholegrain and 1 cup all-purpose)
4 tsp baking powder
1 tbsp sugar
¾ tsp salt
¼ cup cold butter, cut into small pieces
⅓–⅔ cup milk (depending on the wholegrain flour you use)
1 egg
1 tbsp water

METHOD

1. Preheat oven to 425°F.
2. In a food processor, add flour, baking powder, sugar, and salt and mix to combine.
3. Add butter, and pulse until mixture gets crumbly. With the machine running, drizzle in enough milk to bring the dough together.
4. Turn onto a lightly floured surface and fold gently about four times, just until the dough

comes together. Roll or pat down to a one-inch thickness. Using a small cutter, punch out 12 biscuits, rerolling scraps as necessary. Or with a knife, slice the dough into 12 pieces.

5. Combine egg and water in a small bowl and whisk to break yolk.

6. Place biscuits on a parchment-lined baking sheet and lightly brush tops of biscuits with egg wash.

7. Bake for 10 to 12 minutes or until lightly browned. Remove from oven and allow to cool slightly. Spread with butter and jam, then donate some money to a community food centre so that other people can enjoy treats fresh from the oven too.

JOSHNA'S EGG SALAD SANDWICH

MAKES 2

This is my favourite way to eat egg salad. It's got big, bright flavour and crunchy bits to keep things interesting. Add what you like, but for god's sake, spread that filling to the furthest edges of the bread, please!

INGREDIENTS

4 hard cooked eggs, peeled
⅓ cup mayonnaise
2 scallions, finely chopped
1 tbsp fresh parsley, finely chopped
a few dashes of hot sauce, like Tabasco or Frank's
juice from ½ lemon
kosher salt
freshly cracked black pepper
4 slices multigrain bread
1 cup watercress or arugula

METHOD

1. Place eggs in a medium mixing bowl and chop using a pastry blender or potato masher until the pieces are the size of a pencil eraser.
2. Add mayonnaise, scallions, parsley, hot sauce, lemon juice, salt, and pepper and mix gently to combine. Taste and adjust seasoning as necessary.
3. Lightly toast bread. Lay down two slices of toast

and spread each slice with half of the mixture. Top each sandwich with half of the greens, then the other piece of toast, and press down lightly.

4. Slice sandwich, enjoy, and then take your full belly out to volunteer your time at a food bank, hospital, or community food centre.

ACKNOWLEDGEMENTS

Gratitude to . . .

Dad for being my number one fan.

Mom for teaching me to be fearless and work hard.

Ajay for always being there with me, in my corner.

Aunty Lita for teaching me the deep joy of feeding people.

Aunty Ruth for introducing me to the magic of a recipe.

Aunty Kay for showing me how to love people with food.

My editor, Jen Knoch. You are gift from above. Thank you for planting this seed and tending to it so lovingly. I could not have asked for better hands and heart to share this process with. Your name should be right on the cover beside mine.

The smart and wonderful team at ECW Press for helping me get these stories and big ideas out into the world.

My 310 Kickstarter contributors and all of the lovely people who supported my campaign in kind. This book would not exist without you.

Sarah Crawford for passionately convincing me in a lineup for drinks how much I needed to write this book when I was having second thoughts.

My colleagues and community at The Stop, past and present. I hold you all, and that place, very dearly in my heart.

Anne Marie Males, Susan Bull, Debbie Lennox, and the team in Nutrition and Food Services at The Scarborough Hospital. And to Tracy Maccarone, Shawn Studholme, and the team in Nutrition and Food Services at SickKids Hospital. You all took a chance and jumped into the deep end with me, and I'll always be grateful for that. We learned so much together, and those lessons are in the bones of this book.

John Horne, Jason Bangerter, and Oliver & Bonacini Restaurants for your very generous support of this work and your exemplary hospitality.

Julia Hanigsberg for your vision, leadership, and perpetual readiness to fix what's not working.

Melissa Yu Vanti for your deep commitment to your values and doing things well. And for your leadership, impeccable attention to detail, and general cleverness.

John Corallo, David Folkerth, Rossy Earle, Rory Gallagher, Silvana Babikian, Anna Lianos, and the

Ryerson Eats team for joining me on this crazy ride with such openness and so much hard work and commitment to making change.

Ashlee Collins, Geetha Ramasamy, David McGann, Tyler Watson, Mike Masse, Saajid Khan, Hadi Chahin, Kevin Booth, Lorna Willis, Eli Browne, Therese D'Souza, Niveen Saleh, Jay Diwash, and the Chartwells/ Compass Group team for being open to doing things differently and for putting up with my constant adjustments and requests.

John Austin, Jen Gonzales, Brandon Smith, Ian Crookshank, Troy Murray, and the team at Ryerson Student Affairs for your allyship and constant support. And to all of my Ryerson colleagues for your consistent enthusiasm about what we were trying to build.

Kareem Rahaman, Hamza Khan, Bailey Parnell, Janakan Srimurugan, and the Splash Effect team for keeping our web presence fresh and our socials sharp.

Andrew McAllister, Eric Newstadt, Rejean Hoilett, and the Ryerson Students' Union for pushing for change.

Ryerson students for opening your hearts and mouths to a new food culture and for constantly challenging me.

Burkhard Mausberg, Namgyal Dolker, Franco Naccarato, Kathy MacPherson, and the team at the Greenbelt Fund. All of this was only possible with your support, and just look at what we've done together!

Jamie Kennedy and Donna Dooher for seeing what I've been trying to do and for your generosity and mentorship over so many years.

My chef and food community, here and around the world. We're in this together, and I am so grateful for your inspiration and solidarity.

Grace Mandarano, Paul Sawtell, Gill Flies, and Brent Preston for your deep shared values, your incredible support of my work, sweet friendship, and classified conversations. In so many ways, this is our story.

My incredible community of farmers and producers in Southern Ontario for your hard work and your loyalty, for enduring the disappointments, and for always being ready to try to make it work.

My cousin Nathan, for being a magical combo of trusted expert, coach in my corner, and brother from another mother.

My people, my friends who are family, for a whole lifetime of love, support, and laughs that make my face hurt. You all take good care of me.

All of my kiddos for being a source of deep-in-the-belly joy. We're rebuilding this food system for you and your kiddos.

These folks have offered education, inspiration, and support and have helped me create and shape the ideas and stories on these pages, and they need individual mentions: Raj Patel, Sean Sherman, Michael Pollan, Danny Meyer, Jamie Oliver, Wayne Roberts, Vandana Shiva, Alice Waters, Paul DeCampo, Shamek Pietucha, Tatum Wilson, Kevin Gallagher, Janice Sorenson, Hayley Lapalme, Leslie Carson, Peter Mitchell, Rod Bowers, Jessica Leeder, Lulu Cohen and David Farnell, Wendy Smith, Beth Hunter,

Michael Forbes, Glenn Kitchener, Kat Gibson, Laila Emir, David Hertz, Norberto Caceres, Valerie Howes, Zainab Jamal, Angela Warburton, Jennifer Reynolds, Paul Taylor, Tony Conte, Ayal Dinner, Meredith Hayes, Brooke Zeibell, Charles Levkoe, Jesse Finkelstein, Katie German, Diana Bronson, Ruth Klahsen, Twyla Campbell, Chaiti Seth, Mark Brand, Joanne Bays, The McConnell Foundation, Suzanne Barr, Maria Canabal, Bee Wilson, Dino Paoletti, Andrea Most, Harriet Friedmann, Fiona Yeudall, Mustafa Koc, Denise O'Neill-Green, Lovely Charo, Dan Berger, Bryan and Cathy Gilvesy, Michael Hurley and CUPE, Gill Deacon, Matt Galloway, James Rebanks, Roz Heintzman, Ricky Casipe, Leila Mirshak, Jodi Lastman, Mark Freeman, @slackdoodle, Sheena McIntosh, Ken Steele, Dave Kranenburg, Mark Kenny, Sylvain Charlebois, Studio Olafur Eliasson, Victoria Elliasdottir, Ursula Heinzelmann, Oz Zafar, Arlene Stein, Lori Stahlbrand, Chris Trussell, Katy Weber, Jesse Eaton Russell, Carl Heinrich, Ryan Donovan, and sweeeeet Brad Long!

This land was and is inhabited by diverse Indigenous communities. The institutions mentioned in this book all stand on the traditional territory of many nations, and I am grateful for the space to do this work. I am learning how to use my work to meaningfully incorporate Indigenous wisdom, food, and traditions into the culture and organization of our public institutions. I think that the institutional kitchen is an essential site for the big work of decolonization.

The patients, residents, students, and prisoners enduring those dismal meals, and the incredible teams of food service staff everywhere, working hard to do the best they can with what they've got. A better food future is in our grasp, friends, and I'll keep working to get it right.

And finally, to you, dear reader. Thanks for reading this book! I hope you feel inspired to take some action. Think about what you can do in your community to build better connections between people and food, then go and do it! We need all the hands we can get.

SELECTED SOURCES

INTRODUCTION

Canadian Press. "Study Links Diet of Ultra-Processed Foods to Chronic Disease Risk." *CBC News*, June 27, 2019, cbc .ca/news/health/ultra-processed-foods-chronic-disease-risk-1.5192471.

"Conference Proceedings." *The True Cost of American Food — April 14–17 2016, San Francisco*. Sustainable Food Trust, April 2016, sustainablefoodtrust.org/wp-content/ uploads/2013/04/TCAF-report.pdf.

"Facts & Figures — Publicly Funded Home Care." Home Care Ontario, homecareontario.ca/home-care-services/ facts-figures/publiclyfundedhomecare. Accessed Oct. 14, 2019.

Fassler, Joe, and Claire Brown. "Prison Food Is Making U.S. Inmates Disproportionately Sick." *The Atlantic*, Dec. 27, 2017, theatlantic.com/health/archive/2017/12/prison-food-sickness-america/549179.

Health Fact Sheets. "Fruit and Vegetable Consumption, 2017."
Statistics Canada, April 30, 2019, www150.statcan.gc.ca/
n1/pub/82-625-x/2019001/article/00004-eng.htm.

Murphy, Tracy. "The Role of Food in Hospitals."
*HealthCare*CAN, May 2017, healthcarecan.ca/wp-content/
themes/camyno/assets/document/Reports/2017/HCC/
EN/RoleofFood_FinalEN.pdf.

Santo, Alysia, and Lisa Iaboni. "What's in a Prison Meal?"
The Marshall Project, July 7, 2015, themarshallproject.org/
2015/07/07/what-s-in-a-prison-meal.

"Sean Sherman at 2018 World of Flavors." *YouTube*, April
22, 2018, youtu.be/1oRoy6o8LWA.

Xie, Edward. "Bring on the Hospital Food." *Canada's
National Observer*, May 17, 2019, nationalobserver.com/
2019/05/17/opinion/bring-hospital-food.

CHAPTER 1: GOOD FOOD VALUES

Allen, Patricia. "Realizing Justice in Local Food Systems."
Cambridge Journal of Regions, Economy and Society, vol. 3,
no. 2, July 2010, pp. 295–308. doi.org/10.1093/cjres/rsq015.

"Carbon Farming." *Carbon Cycle Institute*, 2019, carboncycle
.org/carbon-farming.

"Climate Change and Land." Intergovernmental Panel on
Climate Change (IPCC), Aug. 6, 2019, ipcc.ch/report/
srccl.

Econometric Research Limited, Harry Cummings &
Associates, and Rod MacRae. "Dollars & Sense:
Opportunities to Strengthen Southern Ontario's Food
System." Greenbelt Foundation, Jan. 2015, greenbelt.ca/
dollars_and_sense_opportunities_2015.

Hawken, Paul, editor. *Drawdown: The Most Comprehensive*

Plan Ever Proposed to Reverse Global Warming. New York: Penguin, 2017.

Irfan, Umair. "Report: We Have to Change How We Eat and Grow Food to Fight Climate Change." *Vox*, Aug. 8, 2019, vox.com/2019/8/8/20758461/climate-change-report-2019-un-ipcc-land-food.

Meyer, Danny. *Setting the Table*. New York: HarperCollins, 2006.

Ray, Deepak K., Paul C. West, Michael Clark, James S. Gerber, Alexander V. Prishchepov, and Snigdhansu Chatterjee. "Climate Change Has Likely Already Affected Global Food Production." *PLoS ONE*, May 31, 2019. doi.org/10.1371/journal.pone.0217148.

Weber, Christopher L., and H. Scott Matthews. "Food-Miles and the Relative Climate Impacts of Food Choices in the United States." *Environmental Science & Technology*, vol. 42, no. 10, April 16, 2008, pp. 3508–3513. doi.org/10.1021/es702969f.

CHAPTER 2: COMMUNITY FOOD CENTRES

Allen, Patricia. "Realizing Justice in Local Food Systems." *Cambridge Journal of Regions, Economy and Society*, vol. 3, no.2, May 14, 2010, pp. 295–308. doi.org/10.1093/cjres/rsq015.

Goodman, Jane, and Claire Conway. "Poor Health: When Poverty Becomes Disease." University of California San Francisco, Jan. 6, 2016, ucsf.edu/news/2016/01/401251/poor-health-when-poverty-becomes-disease.

"Household Food Insecurity in Canada." PROOF: Food Insecurity Policy Research, Feb. 22, 2018, proof.utoronto.ca/food-insecurity.

"New Study Finds Poor Diet Kills More People Globally than Tobacco and High Blood Pressure." Institute for Health Metrics and Evaluation, April 3, 2019, healthdata .org/news-release/new-study-finds-poor-diet-kills-more-people-globally-tobacco-and-high-blood-pressure.

"The Stop's 2018 Annual Report." The Stop, 2018, thestop.org/ wp-content/uploads/The-Stop-2018-Annual-Report.pdf.

"What Is Food Insecurity?" Hunger + Health, 2019, hungerandhealth.feedingamerica.org/understand-food-insecurity.

CHAPTER 3: HOSPITALS

Allard, J., H. Keller, K. Jeejeebhoy, M. Laporte, D. Duerksen, L. Gramlich, H. Payette, et al. "Contributors and Effect of Malnutrition on Length of Stay in Hospital." Canadian Nutrition Society, 2019, nutritioncareincanada.ca/ sites/default/uploads/files/Malnutrition-at-Hospital-Admission.pdf.

"CHEO Spreading the Word about Its Kid-Focused Hospital Menu." *CBC News*, May 26, 2019, cbc.ca/news/canada/ ottawa/hospital-food-cheo-menu-children-recovery-choice-1.5144556.

Crawford, Blair. "Queensway Carleton Proves Hospital Food Doesn't Need to Be Bland." *Ottawa Citizen*, July 18, 2016, ottawacitizen.com/news/local-news/ queensway-carleton-proves-hospital-food-doesnt-need-to-be-bland.

"Food Waste in European Healthcare Settings." Health Care without Harm Europe, Oct. 2016, noharm-europe .org/sites/default/files/documents-files/4336/HCWH Europe_FoodWaste_Flyer_Oct2016.pdf.

Gooch, Martin V., and Abdel Felfel. "'$27 Billion'
    Revisited: The Cost of Canada's Annual Food Waste."
    Value Chain Management International, Dec. 10, 2014,
    vcm-international.com/wp-content/uploads/2014/12/
    Food-Waste-in-Canada-27-Billion-Revisited-
    Dec-10-2014.pdf.

Gunders, Dana. "Hospital Wastes a Third Less Food After
    This One Change." *Forbes*, Feb. 18, 2019, forbes.com/
    sites/danagunders/2019/02/18/hospital-wastes-a-third-
    less-food-after-this-one-change/#6f210dd418c4.

Johnson, Rhiannon. "'Food Is Medicine': Sioux Lookout
    Hospital Program Brings Traditional Foods to Patients."
    Sioux Lookout Meno Ya Win Health Centre, Dec. 26,
    2018, slmhc.on.ca/news/content/articles/article/
    food-is-medicine.

Malhotra, Aseem, Rita F. Redberg, and Pascal Meier.
    "Saturated Fat Does Not Clog the Arteries: Coronary
    Heart Disease Is a Chronic Inflammatory Condition, the
    Risk of Which Can Be Effectively Reduced from Healthy
    Lifestyle Interventions." *British Journal of Sports Medicine*,
    vol. 51, no.15, Aug. 1, 2017, pp. 1111–1112. bjsm.bmj.com/
    content/51/15/1111.citation-tools.

McWilliam, Susannah. "Healthy and Sustainable Hospital
    Food at Gentofte Hospital, Copenhagen." *Food for Life*,
    Oct. 27, 2016, foodforlife.org.uk/whats-happening/
    schools/news-and-blogs/ffl-blog-0000/Gentofte-
    Hospital-Visit.

Murphy, Tracy. "The Role of Food in Hospitals."
    *HealthCare*CAN, May 2017, healthcarecan.ca/wp-content/
    themes/camyno/assets/document/Reports/2017/HCC/
    EN/RoleofFood_FinalEN.pdf.

"The Nourish Program." Nourish, nourishhealthcare.ca/
about-nourish. Accessed Oct. 14, 2019.

Williams, Peter, and Karen Walton. "Plate Waste in Hospitals
and Strategies for Change." *European e-journal of Clinical
Nutrition and Metabolism*, vol. 6, no. 6, Oct. 24, 2011,
e235–e241. Clinical Nutrition ESPEN: doi.org/10.1016/
j.eclnm.2011.09.006.

CHAPTER 4: COLLEGES AND UNIVERSITIES

"AASHE Campus Sustainability Hub." Association for the
Advancement of Sustainability in Higher Education, hub.
aashe.org/browse/topics/purchasing/. Accessed Oct. 14,
2019.

"Average Farmer Hourly Pay in Canada." PayScale, payscale
.com/research/CA/Job=Farmer/Hourly_Rate. Accessed
Oct. 14, 2019.

Cardinal, Brad. "Study: College Students Not Eating
Enough Fruits and Veggies." Oregon State University,
Aug. 17, 2011, today.oregonstate.edu/archives/2011/
aug/study-college-students-not-eating-enough-fruits-
and-veggies.

Friedman, Zack. "Student Loan Debt Statistics in 2019: A
$1.5 Trillion Crisis." *Forbes*, Feb. 25, 2019, forbes.com/
sites/zackfriedman/2019/02/25/student-loan-debt-
statistics-2019/#d386431133fb.

Henry, Michele. "Ryerson Spending Millions to Cover Food
Conglomerate Aramark Canada's Losses." *Toronto
Star*, Feb. 13, 2013, thestar.com/life/2013/02/13/
ryerson_students_stage_food_fight_for_lower_prices_
better_grub.html.

"Hospitality Services Wins Local Food Award." University

of Guelph, Feb. 28, 2012, news.uoguelph.ca/2012/02/
hospitality-services-wins-local-food-award.

Lee, Bruce. "College Foods Needs to Get Better, This PHA
Initiative Is Helping." *Forbes*, Sept. 2, 2018, forbes.com/
sites/brucelee/2018/09/02/college-food-needs-to-get-
better-this-pha-initiative-is-helping/#6ee143de4d0a.

Vomiero, Jessica. "Canadian Students Owe $28B in
Government Loans, Some Want Feds to Stop Charging
Interest." *Global News*, May 31, 2018, globalnews.ca/
news/4222534/canadian-student-loans-government-
interest.

Water Docs. "10 Things You Need to Know About Bottled
Water — and Why You Should Stop Buying It." Ecologos,
April 7, 2018, waterdocs.ca/water-talk/2018/4/7/facts-
about-bottled-water.

CHAPTER 5: SOCIAL GASTRONOMY

Andrés, José. *We Fed an Island: The True Story of Rebuilding
Puerto Rico, One Meal at a Time*. New York: HarperCollins,
2018.

Turshen, Julia. *Feed the Resistance*. San Francisco: Chronicle
Books, 2017.

CONCLUSION

Bauer, Kathleen. "Rosalinda Guillen Is a Force for
Farmworker Justice." *Civil Eats*, July 1, 2019, civileats
.com/2019/07/01/rosalinda-guillen-is-a-force-for-farm-
worker-justice.

"Community Food Security?" FoodARC, foodarc.ca/our-
approach-food-security/community-food-security,
Accessed Oct. 14, 2019.

Nittle, Nadra. "Boston Brings Sustainability, Equity to Its Food Purchasing." *Good Food Purchasing Program*, June 11, 2019, goodfoodcities.org/boston-brings-sustainability-equity-to-its-food-purchasing.

JOSHNA MAHARAJ is a chef, two-time TEDx speaker, and activist. She believes strongly in the power of chefs and social gastronomy to bring hospitality, sustainability, and social justice to the table. Joshna is a regular guest on CBC Radio, a passionate public speaker, and co-hosts *Hot Plate*, a food and drink podcast. She was the recipient of Restaurants Canada's Culinary Excellence Award in 2018.